The Step-by-Step
PAPIER MÂCHÉ
GARDEN

The Step-by-Step

PAPIER MÂCHÉ GARDEN

David Papworth

SIMON & SCHUSTER

LONDON · SYDNEY · NEW YORK · TOKYO · SINGAPORE · TORONTO

Text: David Papworth
Editor: Fleur Robertson
Design and Typesetting: Stonecastle Graphics Ltd
Photography: John Glover, Neil Sutherland
Production Director: Gerald Hughes
Production: Ruth Arthur, Sally Connolly, Neil Randles,
        Jonathan Tickner

The publishers would like to thank Lady Heald, of
Chilworth Manor, and Mr and Mrs P. R. Styles of
Brookwell for granting permission to photograph
papier mâché models in their gardens.

CLB 4025
This edition published in 1995 by Simon & Schuster
© 1995 CLB Publishing, Godalming, Surrey.
Printed and bound in Singapore
ISBN 0-671-71434-1

CONTENTS

INTRODUCTION

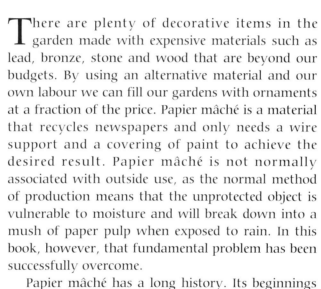

There are plenty of decorative items in the garden made with expensive materials such as lead, bronze, stone and wood that are beyond our budgets. By using an alternative material and our own labour we can fill our gardens with ornaments at a fraction of the price. Papier mâché is a material that recycles newspapers and only needs a wire support and a covering of paint to achieve the desired result. Papier mâché is not normally associated with outside use, as the normal method of production means that the unprotected object is vulnerable to moisture and will break down into a mush of paper pulp when exposed to rain. In this book, however, that fundamental problem has been successfully overcome.

Papier mâché has a long history. Its beginnings were in the Far East, where it was used as a base for lacquer work. It reached Europe in the eighteenth century and quickly caught on as a means of recycling expensive paper into useful objects. Originally based on repulped paper mixed with glue or paste into a purée that is then pressed into moulds or used as a modelling compound, the process developed using sheets of paper glued together and pressure moulded into trays, buttons ornamental mouldings, figurines and even small items of furniture. These items were usually covered with lacquer or oil-based paints to seal the surface from moisture and proved very successful.

8

Papier mâché was used in the 18th century at Painshill Park in Surrey to construct figures set in a pediment on a classical style building as a low cost substitute for marble sculptures. Papier mâché is not normally associated with exterior use but if prepared correctly will stand up to the weather. My family has had a papier mâché baby's bath in use for three generations and would still be using it for the fourth but an adult unfortunately sat on it, damaging it beyond repair. It was simply a thick layer of papier mâché protected inside and out with numerous coats of paint.

Pots, urns and tubs for plants have been in use, either to contain invasive varieties or to grow tender subjects that can be lifted indoors for the winter, for centuries. Statues, seats, obelisks, buildings and balustrades have all added scale, dignity and style to garden settings. These items cost a small fortune, particularly if they are a decent size, but if you make your own with papier mâché the costs are reduced dramatically. The most simple method to construct these items is to have a wire framework to act as a skeleton and form a base on which to build the papier mâché. Additional protection is given by waterproofing the surface with a proprietary product before decorating which means that should the skin of paint be pierced, the papier mâché will not deteriorate with moisture. The papier mâché models are light in weight in proportion to their size, easy to move around the garden and in some cases need to be anchored to stop them being blown about by the wind.

The object of this book is to provide new ideas for the garden rather than to copy existing garden ornaments. It is designed to show you how to make fun objects with a touch of humour or whimsy, so you can have various beasts out of context or larger than life to make a spectacle and spring a surprise with the unexpected. Readers are encouraged to use this book as a stimulus to expand into other areas and to use their imaginations, but whatever you wish to make it is wise to start with something small to get used to handling the materials. You will then have the confidence to tackle larger objects.

PAPIER MÂCHÉ

To keep the method of construction of these models as simple as possible, only one basic system is used in this book, with variations only where really necessary. The common method uses a skeleton formed with wire that is tied together with finer wire. This is then covered over with chicken wire, which in turn makes a base for the papier mâché. Once the framework is covered with the papier mâché it is treated with a waterproofing solution and then decorated. Obviously sizes of models vary and some will need more strength built into their structure than others.

TO START

For all the models you will need a ruler and a pencil or felt-tip pen to measure and mark the wire. Wire comes in a variety of thicknesses called gauges, so for simplicity just three gauges have been selected. For the larger models and where strength is required 4 millimetre diameter wire is chosen as it is the thickest that can be comfortably bent with the hands. Two millimetre wire is much easier to manipulate into shape and is used for small items and where sharp details are needed such as teeth and claws. The .9mm wire is thin and very flexible so this is used to tie the other wires together. Use galvanised wire to give the model a long life free from rust and corrosion. When tying the frame together it is necessary to neatly twist the fine wire completely round the thicker wires to minimise the danger of being scratched by the sharp ends of the fine wire. This rule is important to follow because as one proceeds the apertures become smaller and this is the time when fingers are squeezing between wires to form the whole shape. These wires are sold in coils and usually by weight rather than length and have to be cut by the purchaser into sections for use. A pair of medium-duty bolt cutters is ideal for the thicker 4 and 2mm wires

A grizzly bear is far easier to make than it appears, yet looks extremely impressive when set in place in the garden. See page 68!

while the thinner .9mm wire is easily cut with a pair of diagonal side nippers. When cutting wire and also while forming their shape always allow plenty of space in which to wield long lengths. Bolt cutters leave sharp ends to the wire that can scratch the unwary, so take care by wearing gloves and* bending the ends out of harm's way. Bending the wire needs a firm grip to prevent it slipping so combination and long-nose pliers are ideal for making accurate angles.

THE FRAMEWORK

The framework has a covering of chicken wire to form the ground for the papier mâché to cover. This mesh comes in a variety of sizes, lengths and widths of roll. For our purposes the main yardstick is whether you can get your fingers through the netting to bend and manipulate it – a 25mm (1in) mesh is a good all round size and, if it has a width of 900mm (36in) or 1060mm (42in), it is ideal. Wider rolls become more unwieldy while narrower ones will mean more joins. The length of roll will depend on the size of model and how many you are going to make: if you are making just one small item then a large roll is uneconomical, it is better to buy a short roll. It costs more per metre or yard but the short length that you require still makes it cheap. The diagonal side nippers will cut through the chicken wire without strain and here, again, the wire ends are sharp. The chicken wire can be moulded by squeezing the hexagon holes out of shape by stretching or making them narrower. The mesh can partially pre-formed before applying to the framework. Additional modelling and trimming can be undertaken to obtain the desired effect, but always make sure that sharp wire ends are carefully bent under and used to anchor the mesh.

APPLYING THE PÂPIER MACHÉ

Once the framework and its covering of chicken wire are complete and satisfactory, make sure that the forms are correct. It is easier to adjust at this stage, whereas beyond this step, it becomes progressively more difficult to change. The papier mâché is very simple to apply, provided one follows simple rules. The first rule is to have ample space, while the second is to have all the materials at hand. The paper is simply torn into strips. You will need a bucket or vessel in which to mix the paste and a brush to spread an even film of paste over the paper. The third rule is to use different coloured newspaper so that you can see each layer as you lay it. This ensures that the paper does not end up being extra thick in one place and too thin in another. Use narrow strips of paper to wind round the object. For the tighter the forms and the smaller the models make the strips narrower in order to mould them round the curves. For a larger model use wider strips. Paper has a grain and you will find that it is easier to tear paper along this grain. It is best to proceed using smaller pieces with all the edges torn as this will blend into a smooth surface without the sharp ridge of a cut edge.

Use a cold water wallpaper paste and a flat board that is covered with a waterproof surface, such as melamine or even a piece of armoured glass, as these are easier to wash afterwards. The paper strips are laid out on the board and pasted, allowing the paste to soak into the paper before the wet strips are laid over the framework. Large models will need to have several strips laid round to form a basic lattice work on which more strips can be laid to cover up all the gaps. Once one layer is complete all over it is important to change the colour of the paper to proceed with the next layer and so on until one has five or six layers. Larger objects and those that are going to be handled a lot should have additional layers to give them extra strength. The models described in this book are not designed as children's playthings and if this use is required it is important to add an additional 4mm wire framework as well as up to twenty layers of papier mâché to stand up to the wear the model could need to take.

THE WATERPROOFING

You need to waterproof the paper using a proprietary brand of liquid sealer suitable for absorbent surfaces. These are normally clear in colour and can be brushed or sprayed on. Where there is access to the interior of the model a spray is by far the best method of reaching between the chicken wire. Here a brush has great difficulty in providing adequate coverage. Some manufacturer's market their own inexpensive spray attachment that fits directly onto their container. Follow the manufacturer's instruction carefully and allow the recommended time to elapse for drying. A coat of acrylic primer covers up the newsprint and gives an excellent surface for the subsequent coats of painted decoration. Always use exterior quality paint to provide excellent weather protection. Invest in a few top quality brushes, they keep their shape, do not loose their hairs while painting and last for a long time. Try wide and medium decorating brushes for large models; hog hair, sable and nylon artists' brushes for medium and small models; and fine pointed brushes for details and lines.

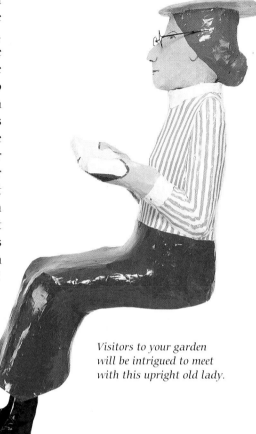

Visitors to your garden will be intrigued to meet with this upright old lady.

Far left: set in the right place, papier mâché models, such as this swan, look extremely effective.

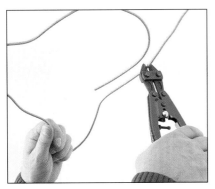

Use galvanised wire to make the frame, choosing a gauge of 4mm to make the larger items where strength and support are needed.

You might prefer the use of gloves to protect your hands from the possibility of scratching, and they lessen the feel of the metal too.

Bend the end of cut wire over at the earliest opportunity to keep it out of harm's way, as it will be sharp and could scratch or catch clothing.

Placing the model in the garden requires careful thought. Most will act either as a focal point or as an unexpected surprise when wandering through the garden if half hidden in the flowers and shrubs. One problem that occasionally occurs is that as papier mâché is light in weight and therefore vulnerable in high winds. Anchoring them with a concrete base is to be recommended, or stakes can be driven into the soil to hold the **model** while in some cases wire extensions can be provided for pushing into the earth, particularly where a permanent position is not wanted. Standard concrete for the foundations is fine, provided there is sufficient concrete above and below the metal anchors attached to the model. Where the concrete base has to be set into water it is necessary to seal the surface to stop salts and chemicals from leaching into the pool. Use a good covering of pond paint and follow the manufacturer's instructions.

WIRING THE FRAME

Treat the wire frame as a skeleton to support and strengthen the whole model. Use galvanised wire to make the frame, which comes in coils of varying lengths and gauges of 4mm, 2mm and .9mm diameters. The thicker wire is used for the large items and where strength and support are required. The 2mm is an infill wire to flesh out the framework and to form the structures for the smaller models, while the thinnest .9mm wire is used to bind and tie the thicker wires together. The thicker wires are measured, marked and then cut using the bolt cutters. As the wire is supplied in coils there is usually some difficulty in measuring round the curve, so a flexible rule is recommended to overcome this problem. The wire will, in most cases, need to be straightened, this is done by bending the wire straight in short lengths at a time. Start at one end and progress along the wire, gently evening out the curve. You will be able to see the wire becoming straight – just keep on lightly taking out the kinks.

When forming the desired shape be aware where the join or overlap is placed, and avoid a join where

the modelling is critical, such as the nose or tail tip. It is far better to make the join along one side where it is less noticeable. In order to make an even curve all the way round a circle of wire, mould the wire round an existing drum, tin or container slightly smaller than the size required. The spring in the wire will enlarge the curve to the correct size. Make sharp angles with two pairs of pliers or use a length of pipe to slide along the wire to the required spot and then form the bend. The pipe will hold the wire straight but do make sure that the pipe is at the free end of the wire and is not captured by the bend. A vice is also very useful in holding the wire, freeing both hands to work on the wire to bend and form it more accurately.

A sharp end is left when you cut the wire and this can scratch your flesh or snag your clothes unless you treat the wire end with great care, filing the sharpness off or bending the end over at the earliest opportunity to keep it out of harm's way. It is wise to place the wire ends close to other wires where the ends are safeguarded, wire ties should be twisted round the frame to curve them close to the larger wire. This also gives a neat finish and makes a better join. You might prefer the use of gloves to protect your hands from the possibility of scratching, and they do lessen the feel of the metal wire when you bend it to shape.

When making some models where there is stretch of leg, support or stem, increasing the wiring or thickness of papier mâché could cause the support to bend. An additional strand of wire or two will hold the model secure. Bind the wires together first with wire, then secondly with papier mâché. If the framework is loosely formed and sways, tighten the joints and if necessary add some crossbracing to make the structure rigid – this is more critical on the larger models where there is more play and flexibility with the frame.

Once the wire frame has been completed the covering of chicken wire is added. The netting is readily cut to size with the diagonal side nippers, but do take care with the sharp wire ends. You can use large pieces of mesh where you have a large model with simple forms, but with the smaller

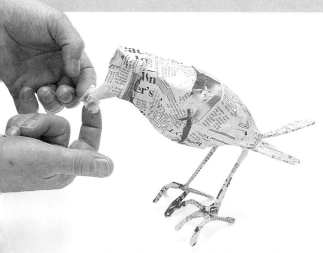

Use smaller pieces of pasted paper for the final coats of papier mâché as this will give a more even finish to the finer details, such as this robin's beak.

models and complicated shapes use smaller pieces; these are easier to handle and to fit to the frame. The chicken wire is simple to form: pull the mesh out of shape and squeeze the hexagons so the flat mesh becomes curved in different directions. Once the rough contours are made the netting is positioned and then squeezed to fit the framework exactly. Surplus wire should be trimmed with the diagonal side nippers. Keep the off-cuts to use for gaps and round the odd protuberances, such as ears and feet. Take care to fold the sharp wire ends under the adjacent netting and round the framework with the long-nose pliers – this will also anchor the mesh firmly in place.

Once the netting is secured to the framework, go over the form and check that the wire has a smooth surface on which to build up the papier mâché covering. Use the long-nose pliers to pull and push the mesh into shape to achieve the desired effect – the narrow tips will reach through the chicken wire to grip the wire ends that are out of reach of the fingers and other kinds of pliers. Take care with the tips of the tails and other pointed forms. Trim some of the wire ends and bend over the tips of the remainder to produce a crisp end with a smooth surface.

PAPIER MÂCHÉ MIXTURE

Papier mâché originated in the Far East where it was used as a base for lacquer work. The early examples used old paper that was reduced to the basic mix of vegetable fibres, and thin glue or size in a soup-like consistency. This was drained and the wet pulp pressed into moulds and allowed to dry. It was then removed and covered with layers of lacquer. This was the method for making boxes, trays and small items of furniture. Over the years the techniques were improved and exported, and in the eighteenth century they reached the West, where they were speedily copied. Trays were made in Europe by glueing sheets of paper together and pressure moulding them into items like trays, buttons, masks and trinkets. Once the mouldings were dry they were coated with a suitable finish to preserve them from moisture. These items were very popular as they were tough, light and relatively cheap.

The method used in this book uses layers of paper stuck together with paste. Using ordinary newspapers recycles paper and makes something from a waste product. Newspaper is a cheap product that uses wood crushed into fibres, mixed with water and then spread over a flat area to drain. The resulting sheet is a rough paper that absorbs liquid easily, can be torn into small pieces or strips, and dries quickly. If the paper is water-proofed and covered with paint to keep out the light and air, the wood fibres should last for years.

The recommended adhesive is a cold water starch wallpaper paste. You can use the cellulose variety or even the heavy duty products for hanging vinyls: what is important is the ability of the paste to soak into the paper to leave a film of adhesive on the surface. If the paste is too thin then the liquid is soaked up by the paper but has little stick on the surface and will soon dry and peel off. If the paste is too thick then it remains on the surface and doesn't sink into the paper and the adhesion is poor. Ideally the paste should be of a creamy consistency that spreads easily without lumps and the paper soon becomes saturated. This is seen by the paper turning a darker colour. Newsprint that features four-colour printing or even a solid black printed area will take longer to soak up the paste and this must be allowed for.

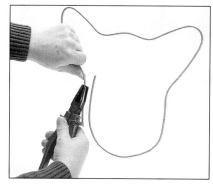

When forming a shape in wire, be aware where the join is placed, avoiding one where the modelling is critical, such as an ear tip.

Bending the wire needs a firm grip to prevent it slipping, so combination and long-nosed pliers are ideal for accurate angles.

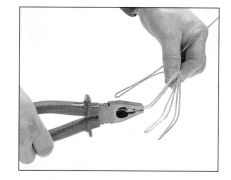

Once the framework is complete, ensure the forms and little details, such as feet, are correct. It is easier to adjust them at this stage than at any other.

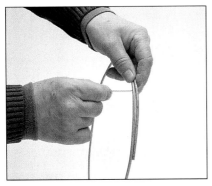

Use .9mm wire – the thinnest gauge wire – to bind and tie the thickest wires together. Take care that no tiny ends are left proud.

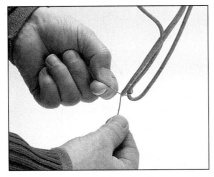

Secure two parts of the wire framework with the thinnest gauge wire, which can easily be manipulated with the hands.

Using pliers, twist the ends of fine binding wire to complete the securing process that keeps two heavier gauge wires together.

Magazine paper can be used but is much less absorbent, slower to soak up the paste and reluctant to dry. The situation is made worst with colour printing as there are four coloured layers to penetrate before the paper is reached. This is one area where the tabloids can lord it over the quality broadsheets, the cheaper the paper the more superior it is for this method of papier mâché. Paper that has a colour additive helpful in monitoring the coverage and number of coats by laying alternate colour and white paper coats.

There are parts of models where it is necessary to build up areas with a ridge or spot to emphasise a characteristic form. Here a pulp system is used. This entails tearing newspaper up into tiny pieces and soaking them in water overnight. In the morning a good stir with a wooden spoon or even putting the mix into a mechanical liquidiser will reduce the pieces to pulp. Partially strain off the water and replace it with some wallpaper paste that is fairly liquid, and then mix thoroughly. Strain off the liquid to leave a soggy heap of pulp that is then positioned onto the model and formed into the desired shape. If the pulp is still too fluid, squeeze it by hand to remove as much liquid as possible. You should now be able to mould it with a modelling tool into the shape you require. It will take quite a while to dry, particularly if it very thick and wet.

PAPIER MÂCHÉ APPLICATION

The wire framework is the base upon which the papier mâché covering is built. The frame surface needs to be smooth and free from projecting wires and sharp edges that could poke through the covering. For a large model with a simple cylindrical or flat form use wide strips of torn paper – these can be up to 150mm (6in) wide. Allow for an overlap of at least 12mm (½in) in each direction. More complicated forms will need narrow strips: experience will soon show where creases appear and where, therefore, you need to make the strips more narrow to give a smooth surface. Use smaller pieces of pasted paper for the final coats as this will give a more even finish.

Use a smooth impervious board to paste on, a sheet of armoured glass or melamine laminate is ideal as they are easily washed after use. The strips of paper are pasted and left to absorb the paste for a few minutes, then lifted and placed in position. Some larger models will require a lattice of strips strung round the frame: this lattice will hold the areas of the base coat securely as they are being formed. It is wise to make the base coat with coloured paper and then use white paper for the second layer so you will know when you have completely covered the base coat. Following with alternate coloured and white layers so that you can monitor your progress. For small items four coats are the minimum required but for the larger models you will need seven or eight layers to form a rigid covering. These numbers should be more than doubled if the model is going to be used for children's toys.

The paper fibres lie mainly in one direction and as they absorb moisture will swell across their width rather than along their length, so, likewise, the strips of paper will expand across the strip and then shrink back to shape. To counteract this allow a good overlap along the length of the strip so that it will dry tight as a drum and not slip and leave a gap. For additional strength lay alternate coats of paper at right angles to the last one like plywood. This will bind the fibres and strips into a thick covering all pulling in different directions and thereby giving a taut and tough covering.

For small areas and tight curves use very narrow strips – and short lengths are easier to manoeuvre than long ones. In places difficult to reach, the use of modelling tools and a bone folder is recommended to move the pieces of paper into position, mould them round small forms and reach into narrow crevices to firm the surface. The pointed ends are ideal for modelling the papier mâché round fingers, claws and teeth, as well as reaching down 'throats'. The edge of the folder is recommended for accentuating the creases and sharp angles on the model, while the broad side of the bone folder is very suitable for smoothing large flat surfaces.

The papier mâché surface is very vulnerable to damage while it is still thin and moist, so great care should be taken while working on it, particularly at the beginning. It is easy to pierce the surface with a sharp instrument and even the finger can poke a hole through it. As the layers are added and the paper dries out the skin becomes much tougher and more rigid. You will probably need to work on one side of the model while the other is still wet. This is fine provided you lay the model on an impervious surface that will not stick to the pasted paper. American cloth, a laminate surface or even a sheet of plastic is adequate. Models with curved surfaces are difficult to hold steady and require some wedging to keep the model from rocking about, while smaller items can be placed in a cup-shaped vessel such as a bucket to act like an egg-cup. Make sure that the size is suitable to hold the model secure while you are working on the papier mâché.

Large objects are often too big to work on in the average room and could cause a domestic crisis! The garage can be used if there is adequate light, otherwise you have to work out of doors. This is fine provided the weather is dry and there is no wind to blow the strips of paper about the garden. An open-sided shed or summerhouse is ideal for

drying the model as it allows the passage of air but protects against the rain.

The use of paper pulp is sometimes necessary to emphasise the character of the model particularly where small areas need additional modelling such as facial details. Apply this pulp in a moist state and work it into shape with a modelling tool. If the surface is still rough on completion, lay some small pieces of pasted paper over the top to provide a smooth surface for painting. The papier mâché must be thoroughly dry before the waterproofing and painting are undertaken to obtain the maximum benefit from these protective coatings.

WATERPROOFING AND PAINTING

Once the covering of papier mâché on the wire framework is complete and thoroughly dry, the surface is ready for the waterproofing treatment. Waterproofing solutions are proprietary products, clear liquids that are brushed or sprayed onto absorbent surfaces to form a barrier that stops the ingress of water. There are several products on the market and it is essential to follow the manufacturer's instructions to get the best results. The surface of the papier mâché has to be thoroughly covered to ensure the maximum saturation of the liquid, and where there is access to the interior of the model it is best to spray the solution to ensure the best coverage, particularly round the supporting chicken wire. Where there is likely to be some water reaching the interior, make sure that there is an outlet at the lowest point. Pierce the papier mâché covering at this place and thoroughly douse the hole with waterproofing solution. Some manufacturers supply a spray attachment that fits onto their containers that is cheap and efficient. The spray covers the model's surface speedily and is easy to use. Once the waterproofing is complete allow the recommended time to elapse before progressing onto the next stage. Wash the brush and spray thoroughly, follow the manufacturer's instructions with regard to solvents for cleaning.

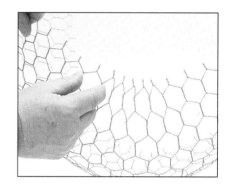

Ensure that you place the wire ends close to other wires – wire ties should be twisted round the frame to curve them close to the larger wire.

Chicken wire is simple to form: pull the mesh out of shape and squeeze the hexagons so the flat mesh becomes curved in different directions.

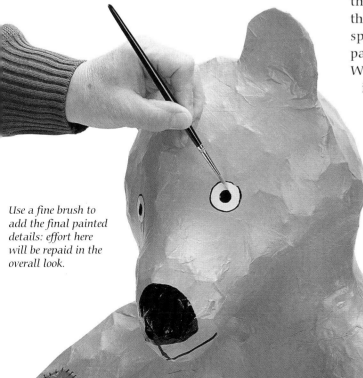

Use a fine brush to add the final painted details: effort here will be repaid in the overall look.

Take care to fold the sharp wire ends under the adjacent netting and round the framework with long nose pliers.

Complicated forms will need the application of short narrow strips of papier mâché to ensure they achieve a smooth surface.

After applying a narrow strip of papier mâché, smooth the surface of the paper down with the hand.

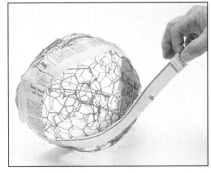

Some larger models will need a lattice of strips strung round the frame: this lattice will hold the areas of the base coat securely.

The waterproofed surface is now ready for the coating of the acrylic primer, which provides a bond between the surface and the decoration. The primer gives a good surface on which to draw out with pencil the areas, shapes and details to be coloured. This primer is usually applied with a wide brush but for smaller models, fine modelling, crevices and creases, use a smaller brush to cover the surface thoroughly without gaps. The brush must be washed out immediately before the primer dries.

When all the areas of colour have been drawn onto the model it is ready to be painted. Use exterior quality paint for the best results – some enamels are suitable but check that they are recommended for exterior use. Where the model is being used for children make sure that the paint is guaranteed free from harmful pigments and oils. To keep the model in pristine condition it is advisable to repaint it every three years or so to keep a protective coating of colour over the papier mâché surface. Apply the paint with the appropriate undercoats and thinners as required by the makers. For a stone effect use a cement paint that has granules of stone in it to provide a texture: several coats are recommended to make a good protective layer. In some cases the use of a spray paint is needed for a particular effect such as weathered stone or shading on an animal skin. Spray paint is available in aerosol cans: a wide range of colours is obtainable for car retouching and they are useful for blending one colour over another. When spraying paint it is advisable to do this in the open, away from naked lights and to wear gloves to avoid ending up with coloured hands!

You will need a selection of brushes to use when painting and there is a wide range from the decorators' bristle, through the artists' hog hair and sable brush to the long pointed nylon fibre liners. Details such as eyes, mouths, spots and lines demand brushes that will give a fine clean line and a long-haired pointed one is ideal for this use. If the paint is at all thick and viscous some thinning is needed to allow a thin brush the ability to give a smooth crisp line and edge.

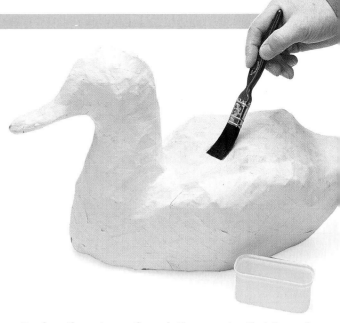

Brush on the waterproofing solution, ensuring that the surface of the papier mâché is entirely covered.

Plan ahead when painting the model so that you can avoid smudging paint on one side while you are painting the other. Some models can be propped up to keep the wet areas away from the ground, while others need to be suspended to allow the paint to dry free from the danger of touching other surfaces. While painting take care that the brush is not overloaded with paint since this can cause runs and drips when applied to the surface of the model. A good brush will spread an even coat over the surface and a vigorous working should spread the paint sufficiently thinly to prevent any accumulation causing a run. When spraying use the paint sparingly to give several thin coats rather than one thick layer that will run towards the bottom of the model. Most aerosol cans give instructions on their use and how far away from the surface they need to be before depressing the button and following these instructions will give the best effect.

FIXINGS

Some models are sufficiently stable and heavy that they can stand without any fixing or they are made with an inbuilt facility to hook or grip onto a tree or branch and remain in position without trouble. Other items however will need some form of anchor to hold them in place and stop them being blown over. There are some models that are designed to have a heavy base of concrete, either to stand in water or on land, some will have a float to keep them above water and others will have spikes to sink into the soil. You will find that there are several papier mâché models with wire extensions to the base to enable them to be moved from place to place round the garden and then are spiked into the ground to hold them secure until the next move.

If you need to keep one of these models in a permanent position the wire extensions can be bent at right angles some 25mm (1in) below the model's base and have a concrete slab formed round these wires. The slab should have at least 25mm (1in) of concrete above and below the wires. Place the model on a sheet of plastic spread over a flat area, and in order to keep the wires from sinking deeper into the concrete, wedge some small pieces of brick or stone under the wires to the correct height. Alternately, suspend it at the right height above the plastic sheet. Concrete is available in bags as a mixture of sand, stones and cement, and all that is required is the addition of water and a thorough mixing. The resulting stiff paste is packed firmly round the wires and outwards to form a slab at least 150mm (6in) beyond them. Leave the model in situ for at least two days before moving to its final site. If the model is large consider whether it can be weighted in this way in its permanent position. You are advised to cover the concrete until it is set to protect it against rain, frost and too-rapid drying. If the concrete slab is visually out of character in your garden you can colour it to blend it into its surroundings.

Where a temporary fixing is required use tent pegs driven into the ground. If the soil is light and sandy you will need a longer spike or even one with an anchor plate to be buried under the earth to secure it. The model is tied to the anchor with a nylon line, chosen because it is strong and thin and virtually invisible. As each garden situation is unique it is difficult to give precise instructions that will fit every case: the size, strength and number of fixings must be decided according to your type of soil and placing of the model, but provide too much anchorage rather than too little. A number of designs are placed in tree situations and have inbuilt hook or are made to grip round the branches or trunk, while some birds have wire claws that are bent to fit the particular branch. If the grip on these is insufficient then additional fixing with nails and nylon line will be required to hold the model secure.

Apart from the obvious places around the garden to place the models you should also consider the use of fences, pergolas and roofs as sites. If you do raise the models up high make sure that they are securely fixed and that the structure that it is being secured to is also safe. Models that have concrete bases that actually stand in the water will need to have the concrete sealed with a pond paint to stop salts and chemicals leaching out into the water and upsetting the balance to the detriment to plant and fish life. The bases have to be positioned on the pond floor carefully to cause no harm to the pond liner, casting or pond sealant – it is advisable to provide a cushion between the base and pool floor with a pad of pond liner or thick rubber matting. Floats are made from cork or expanded polystyrene slabs usually some 25mm (1in) thick. To make the latter more discrete spray the surface with a neutral colour that will blend in with your pond water. If you use a cellulose spray, the surface of the polystyrene will start to dissolve slightly leaving a rough and natural looking finish. If you find that the models with floats always end up drifting into one corner, tether them with a length of nylon line and a stone to act as an anchor.

The models are all designed to be simple, but readers can elaborate and adjust the sizes to suit particular situations. Those with a talent for electricity could wire up models to produce sounds, blink lights or even provide some movement with an electric motor! It is the constructor's imagination that can make these unique models even more spectacular, unusual and personal to the owner. In the end your imagination can be as large as your garden, to the benefit of you both!

Apply the strips of papier mâché to the detailed areas with care. . .

. . .making sure that the outline is retained.

Finally, lay some small pieces of pasted paper down to provide a smooth surface for painting.

Making a
Papier Mâché
CATERPILLAR

I *have yet to meet a gardener who welcomes caterpillars into the garden, yet they are very attractive creatures to look at. Often they have bright and decorative livery and, if they were prevented from eating the vegetation and so raising the blood pressure of gardeners, they would be an asset to the garden scene.*

By enlarging the caterpillar to a giant size of some 1200mm (48in) long and making it out of papier mâché you have a colourful larva without an appetite.

YOU WILL NEED

4mm wire:
two lengths 3050mm (120in) (A)
2mm wire: twelve lengths
915mm (36in) (B)
one length 815mm (32in) (C)
three lengths 710mm (28in) (D)
one length 610mm (24in) (E)
four lengths 665mm (26in) (F)
three lengths 550mm (22in) (G)

.9mm wire:
various short lengths to tie the
framework together

chicken wire:
one piece 550 x 455mm
(22 x 18in) mid section
two pieces 610 x 300mm
(24 x 12in) head and front
one piece 510 x 405mm
(20 x 16in) rear section
380 x 200mm (15 x 8in)
tail section

Bend one A into the side view of the caterpillar without legs. Bind the overlap with fine wire. Form the other A into the top view, check that it fits exactly to the other A and wire them together at the head and tail. Make ten of the B's into cross sections of the body and wire them into place to the two A's, starting at the head end. Bend C, one D and E into cross sections of the tail end and join to A's with fine wire. Form the remaining two B's into side profiles of the back legs and fix in place to the adjoining B's. Make the two D's into side profiles of the front feet and join to neighbouring B's. Bend the F's into front views of the back legs and secure to A's and B's with fine wire. Make the G's into front views of the front legs and fix them to A's and D's.

Cover the framework with chicken wire – you will find it easier to use several small pieces rather than one large piece. Mould it to fit the framework and bend all sharp wire ends out of harm's way as you progress. Trim off surplus netting as you work, keeping it to cover the feet.

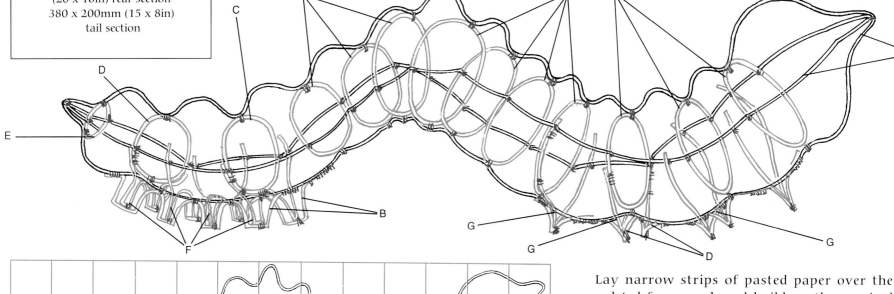

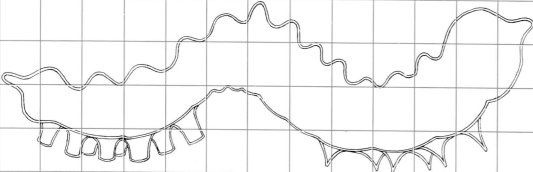

Each square represents 100mm (4 inches)

Lay narrow strips of pasted paper over the completed framework and build up the required coating of papier mâché. Use alternate layers of coloured and white paper to monitor the coverage and thickness. Allow to dry and treat with waterproofing liquid, following the manufacturer's instructions for best results.

Prime the surface and decorate the caterpillar with exterior-quality paint. Position the completed caterpillar in the garden where it will surely prompt admiration rather than annoyance.

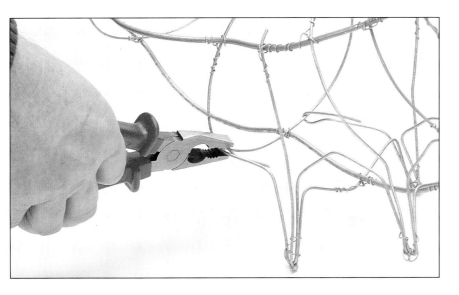

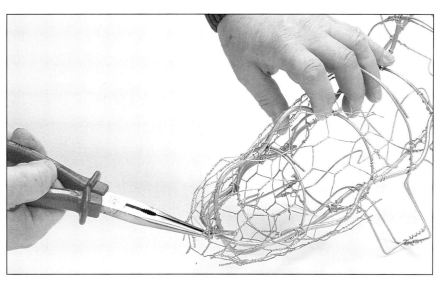

1 Fix the leg wire to the main framework, using the combination pliers to bend over the end of D and anchor it to one of the B's where you can secure it with fine wire.

2 Mould the tail section of chicken wire to fit the framework. Use the long-nose pliers to pull the mesh round the tail, then tuck in loose wire ends to make a smooth form.

3 Cover the legs with short lengths of pasted paper, wind them round the leg and firm them down to provide good adhesion and leave a smooth finish to the surface.

4 Use narrow pieces of paper to cover the feet, rubbing them down with the finger to ensure a good surface. Build up the coat with the strips slightly overlapping each other.

5 Paint the stripes with a fine pointed brush to obtain clean sharp edges. Use the little finger to steady the hand but be careful not to smudge any wet paint.

6 Draw fine lines round the eye with a good quality pointed brush. If the paint is too thick to make a smooth line, dilute it with a little turps so that it flows freely.

Making Papier Mâché FRUIT

*T*o see bunches of luscious outsized grapes
hanging on a vine out of season is a surprise.
Whether in a green house or outside, the
spectacle makes one pause and take a second
look. Make your own oversized succulent fruit
as an original way of decorating your

trees – true, you
can't eat the
fruit, but the
pleasure of seeing
eye-catching and
brilliantly coloured
oranges and really
ripe pears is more
than sufficient.

22

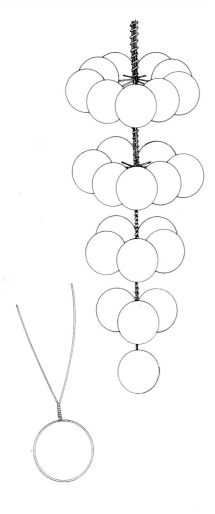

Make each grape from two hemispheres of papier mâché made in easily constructed moulds. Take the lengths of pipe, place on an impervious flat surface and almost fill with modelling clay. Press the ball or knob into the moist clay to leave an imprint that will serve as the mould for the papier mâché. Treat toilet roll tubes with waterproofing solution to stop moisture penetration. A 485g pack of modelling clay will make twelve moulds, enough for six grapes at a time.

Paint the hollow mould with washing-up liquid to prevent the papier mâché sticking to the clay. Line the mould with five layers of tiny pieces of pasted paper; larger pieces will crease. Alternate layers of coloured paper will help you to keep count. Remove the cups of dry papier mâché from the moulds and sort them into pairs, then put them together to make a sphere. Twist a length of wire round each sphere to hold them in place. Lay two coats of pasted paper over the wire and papier

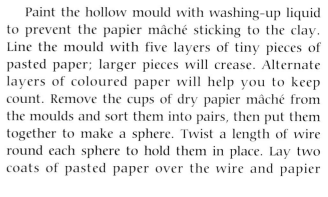

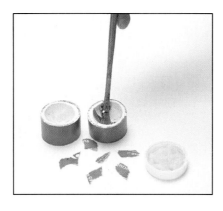

1 *Paste small scraps of paper and line the prepared mould, pushing well down with a stiff brush to squeeze out air bubbles and build up a good layer of papier mâché.*

2 *The dry papier mâché lifts easily out of its mould and the ragged edge is trimmed if necessary to make it mate with the other half.*

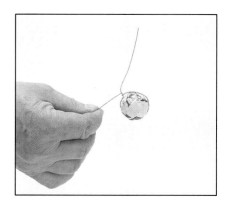

3 *Place the two halves together and twist the wire round. The twisting action will tighten the wire round the papier mâché and hold the sphere firmly.*

4 *Lay further small pieces of pasted paper over the sphere and wire until the whole is covered with two layers. You will find the wires useful to hold as you paste the pieces on.*

5 *Start the bunch with four grapes and twist one of the 'stem' wires round the others to tie the grapes together. Use long-nose pliers to pull the wire taut.*

6 *Add extra rows of grapes and wire to the central stem of the bunch by winding the occasional wire round. Use the long-nose pliers to form a tight bond.*

7 Spray a light dusting of white over the coloured grapes to give the effect of bloom. Use gloves to avoid the drift of paint onto your hands from the aerosol.

mâché to make a grape. When the paper is dry, coat the surface with waterproofing liquid. Hold four grapes by their wires and twist one wire round the 'stem' to form a small bunch. Add extra grapes in rows and continue to wire each row round the stem that is being formed.

Spray primer over the whole bunch and follow with an exterior quality spray paint to give good coverage. This saves poking between the grapes with a wet brush. Colour the grapes green or purple and when dry give a light spray of white to make the bloom on the surface. The bunch is now ready to hang on the vine.

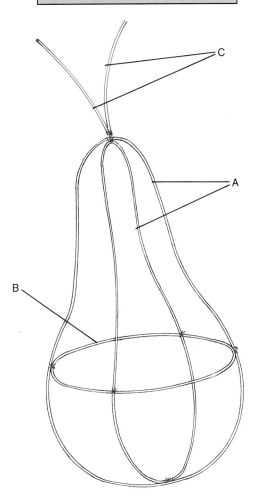

YOU WILL NEED

EACH PEAR:

2mm wire:
two lengths 455mm (18in) (A)
one length 355mm (14in) (B)

.9mm wire:
one length 200mm (8in) (C)
several short lengths for tying the
framework together

chicken wire:
one piece 300 x 200mm
(12 x 8in)

Bend one A to make the side view of the pear 190mm (7½in) long and 90mm (3½in) wide. Bind the overlapping ends together with fine wire. Repeat this shape with the other A but make sure that one will sit inside the other. Place in position and wire the top using C, leaving a length of double wire to attach to the tree. Wire the bottom of A where the wires cross with a short length of fine wire. Form B to make a circle 90mm (3½in) in diameter, position and wire to the two A's.

Bend the chicken wire round the framework, squeeze the top and bottom of the mesh to fit close to the form and trim off surplus wire. Bend over wire ends to give a smooth surface.

Lay narrow strips of pasted paper round the pear to gradually cover the whole surface. This makes the base coat of papier mâché. Continue placing layers of papier mâché until you reach the required thickness then allow to dry thoroughly. Cover the surface with waterproofing solution.

Prime the surface of the pear and paint a base of yellow using exterior-quality paint. To achieve the colourful but irregular blending of the natural pear, use aerosols to spray green at the stem end and red at the other end to provide a look of succulence. The pear is now ready to hang in the tree for a mouth-watering effect.

1 Form the pear shape from length A. Bend the wire to the desired shape and wire the overlapping ends together. Use the combination pliers to grip the wire tightly to form a strong join.

2 Both A's are joined together with fine wire. Use the combination pliers to twist the excess wire round the frame for a neat and safe finish.

3 Bend the chicken wire over the framework and mould to the pear form. Use the diagonal cutting nippers to trim off the surplus wire mesh.

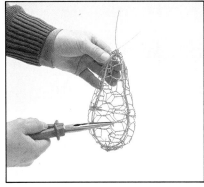

4 Bend over the sharp wire ends and push them under the adjoining mesh and squeeze them flat out of the way. Use the long-nose pliers as they can reach into confined areas.

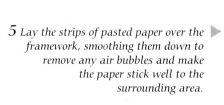

5 Lay the strips of pasted paper over the framework, smoothing them down to remove any air bubbles and make the paper stick well to the surrounding area.

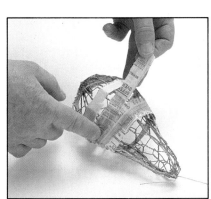

6 *Cover the base coat with the next coat of white paper so that you can see where you have been. Continue with alternate coloured and white layers until the papier mâché is complete.*

7 *Spray on the paint to give a blended effect to the pear. Do this in the open air and, if you don't wish to have coloured hands, wear a pair of gloves for protection.*

W̶ind the length of wire round the ball and twist to give a 'tail' of over 100mm (4in) of double wire. This is used to hook the orange onto the tree. Cover the ball with a layer of papier mâché, starting round the stem area and over the wire to prevent slipping. Use a coloured paper for the base and alternate coats with a white paper layer between these to monitor the number of layers until you reach the desired thickness. Allow the papier mâché to dry thoroughly before treating with the waterproofing liquid.

Paint the surface with primer and follow with exterior-quality bright orange paint to cover the whole orange. When this coat is dry paint the small green star of leaves round the stem area and then colour the tiny black dots to give the skin its characteristic pitted texture. The fruit is now ready to hang up. Either bend the wire into a hook or, where there is a danger of strong winds, twist it round the tree stem to hold the orange secure.

1 *Tie the wire round the ball and twist the ends tight for a good grip on the surface. Use combination pliers to hold and twist the wire, this will tighten it to stop it slipping off.*

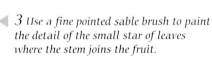

2 *Build up a network of narrow strips of pasted paper over the wire to assist in holding it in place while the rest of the papier mâché is laid.*

3 *Use a fine pointed sable brush to paint the detail of the small star of leaves where the stem joins the fruit.*

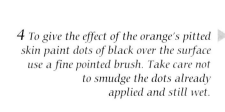

4 *To give the effect of the orange's pitted skin paint dots of black over the surface use a fine pointed brush. Take care not to smudge the dots already applied and still wet.*

YOU WILL NEED

ONE ORANGE:

.9mm wire:
one length 550mm (22in)

one 100mm (4in) diameter
plastic ball

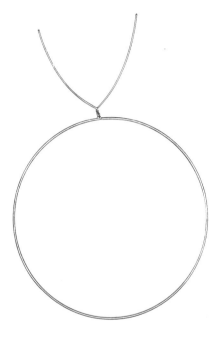

Making a
Papier Mâché
ALLIGATOR

We rarely find reptiles like the alligator or crocodile in a domestic situation – they are very curious and interesting creatures to look at but in real life one doesn't look too closely. Now, though, you can have one as an exotic pet in your pool without incurring any claims for lost limbs. A papier mâché model of an alligator head floating in the pond is an unexpected surprise for most people and a deterrent for paddlers!

YOU WILL NEED

4mm wire:
two lengths 1830mm (72in) (A)
one length 1065mm (42in) (B)
one length 915mm (36in) (C)
three lengths 510mm (20in) (D)
two lengths 405mm (16in) (E)
one length 455mm (18in) (F)

2mm wire:
one length 2700mm (106in) (G)
two lengths 2540mm (100in) (H)
.9mm wire: various short lengths
to tie framework together

chicken wire:
two pieces 760 x 510mm
(30 x 20in)

One piece of 25mm (1in) thick
expanded polystyrene or cork 510
x 300mm (20 x 12in) as float.

Form one A into the plan view of the top jaw and neck and make the other A into the plan view of the lower jaw and neck. Form B into the cross section of the head with eye bulges and join to the A's with fine wire. Bend C into the cross section of the base and wire to the A's. Form one D into a cross section of the nostrils and upper jaw, then secure it in place to A. Make the other two D's into cross sections of the top and bottom jaws near the eyes and fix in place to the A's. Bend E's into the cross sections of both jaws midway along and wire in position. Form F into the front section of the lower jaw and join to A. Manipulate G into the side profile of the head with mouth open and secure to A's, B, C, D's, E and F where the frame crosses with fine wire. Make one H into teeth for the top jaw and the other H for the lower jaw teeth. Bend them into a zig-zag using the pliers to make the sharp angles. Wire both H's to A's with fine wire. Cover the framework with chicken wire, laying one piece on top of the frame, folding it into the

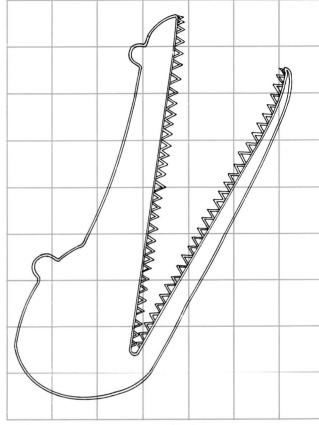

Each square represents 88mm (3½ inches)

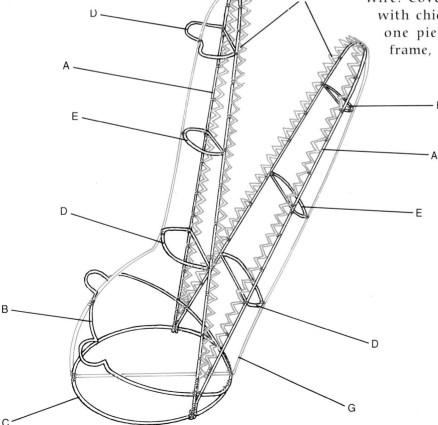

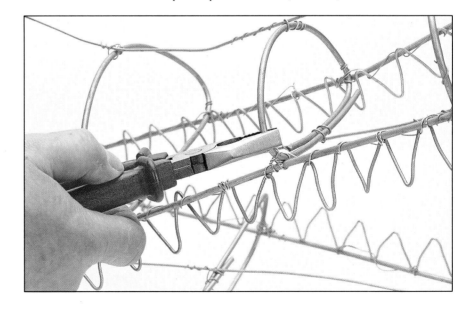

1 Tie the teeth into place with fine wire, wrap the surplus wire round the frame and use the pliers to grip and twist it into place. Avoid the sharp ends of the wires.

mouth and stretching or squeezing the mesh to slide between the teeth. Repeat the process with the other piece of netting round the lower jaw and fold all sharp wires out of harm's way.

Lay strips of paper over the completed framework to build up the papier mâché. Use small pieces to mould round the teeth, keeping the points sharp. When you have reached the required thickness, leave the model to dry before applying the waterproofing solution inside and out. With the latter, follow the manufacturer's instructions carefully for best results.

Prime the surface of the papier mâché and decorate it with exterior-quality paint. Colour the float using a cellulose spray paint on the polystyrene as it will partially dissolve the surface and thereby take on a more weathered appearance. Secure the float to the model with fine wire threaded through the base and round the wire framework. Check that the balance is correct in the water and adjust the float if necessary. You can now launch it onto the pond and see how many children listen intently for the ticking alarm clock.

3 Fold a small piece of pasted paper round each tooth, use a modelling tool to reach into the grooves and between the teeth to fix the papier mâché.

4 Lay strips of pasted paper to build up the inside of the lower mouth. Firm the strips down with the fingers to make a smooth surface to the papier mâché.

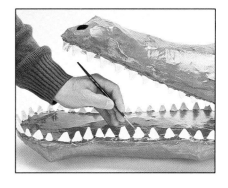

5 Paint the teeth with a fine pointed brush to give a clean sharp edge to the area of white. Start at the throat end and work towards the front to avoid smudging the wet paintwork

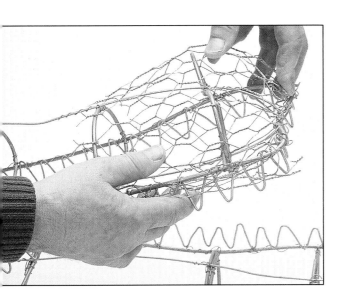

2 Fit the chicken wire round the nose by squeezing and pulling the mesh out of its regular pattern. A short piece is shown for illustration purposes, instead of the larger section.

6 Use the fine brush to paint details of eyes and scales, steady the hand with the little finger to give control.

Making a
Papier Mâché
SNAIL

*D*ull areas in the garden occur between
flowering seasons and where evergreens, which
supply winter colour, look just boring in the
summer months. Brighten up these areas with
a giant colourful snail 600mm (24in)
long and 300mm (12in) high!
Once the garden starts to look
interesting
again it
can easily be
moved to another
dull place. You can
have all the decorative
advantages of a gastropod mollusc, with none
of its destructive disadvantages.

Bend A into the shape of the plan view of the snail, without its tail but with the 125mm (5in) eye stalks, moulding the sides to suggest the undulations of the spiral shell before tying the ends together with the fine wire. Next take B and bend to make the elevation; this is joined to A where the frame wires cross. Form C to make the flat base of the snail, including the tail. Wire the ends together and then fix to B. You now mould D to form the upright round the shell. Wire the ends together, place in position and secure to the main framework. Similarly E and F are formed, positioned and wired in place. The cross section of the head, G, is formed into a circle by bending it round a suitably sized tin and fixing it to A and B.

The framework is now ready to be covered with the chicken wire. You should start with the head, which is easier to form and then follow with the body, which is moulded to form the spiral shell. Surplus mesh is trimmed off and saved to cover the tail area. Fold over all sharp ends to prevent them from piercing the papier mâché covering.

Once the framework is complete it is ready for the papier mâché. You apply this in layers to the required thickness, moulding round the spiral shell forms and allowing to dry thoroughly. Treat the covered snail with the waterproofing solution. It is advisable to spray the interior with the solution to saturate the papier mâché behind the mesh support.

Allow the waterproofing to dry thoroughly before you start painting. Prime and then follow this coat with the exterior paints of your choice. Place the completed snail in position, sit back and wait for complements.

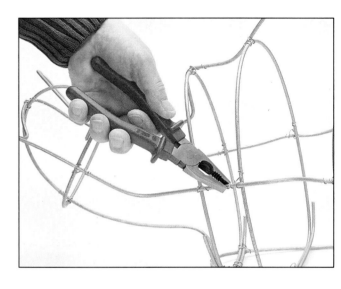

1 Use the combination pliers to twist the fine wire tight, this makes the joints strong and the frame rigid. Wind the surplus fine wire round the frame for neatness and safety.

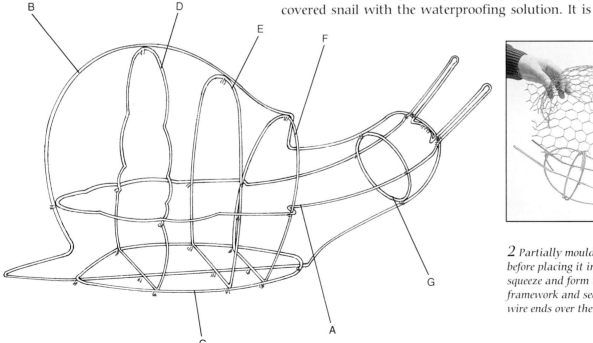

2 Partially mould the chicken wire before placing it in position. Continue to squeeze and form the mesh to fit the framework and secure by twisting the wire ends over the frame.

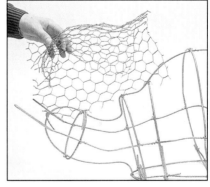

3 Pull wire ends through adjoining mesh with the long-nose pliers to hold them in place; the narrow tips easily reach through the chicken wire to grip and twist the wire.

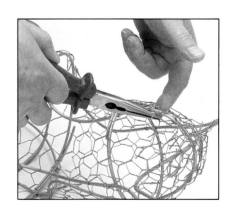

5 *Decorate the surface with exterior paint. Use a small hog hair brush for restricted areas. A good brush gives clean edges to the area of colour.*

4 *Lay alternate coats of papier mâché at right angles to the base coat for strength. Use coloured and white paper to monitor thickness and avoid gaps in each coat.*

6 *Use a fine brush for details and lines. Keep the brush bristles suspended in water or turps between coats to stop the paint drying.*

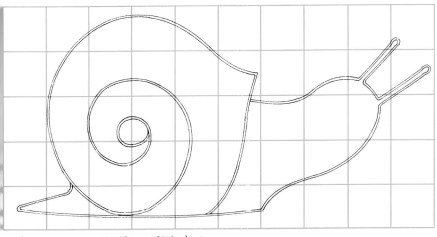

Each square represents 62mm (2½ inches)

Making a
Papier Mâché
OWL

If you have an old tree with a hole, a dark wooded area or an old out-building with a window, consider making the vista more interesting with an owl. This will give you a focal point and provide a source of amusement to your visitors. The owl is simply constructed and the dimensions can be adjusted so that you can make a bird that will fit a particular size of aperture or tree branch.

YOU WILL NEED

4mm wire:
two lengths 1220mm (48in) (A)
one length 840mm (33in) (B)
one length 550mm (22in) (C)

2mm wire:
two lengths 300mm (12in) (D)
two lengths 250mm (10in) (E)

.9mm wire:
various short lengths for tying
the frame

chicken wire:
665 x 535mm (26 x 21in)

Take one A and carefully bend it to form the side view of the owl's body. As the bird is twisted, make it the front view of the head. In bending the wire make the join appear at the side where it can easily be tied together with fine wire. The other A is then bent to form the front view of the body and side elevation of the head, here again the join should be at the side. The two A's are tied together at the top and tail where the wires cross. You now take B and bend into shape. This is best done by forming B round a large tin to make a circle with a diameter of 200mm (8in), with the surplus wire overlapping and the last 50mm (2in) or so bent at right angles to form the centre claws of the feet. B is now wired into place on the main frame. Take C and bend in a similar way to form the neck section with a diameter of 165mm (6½in). This circle is squeezed to form an oval to fit in with the two A's and is tied into place with the fine wire.

Take the two D's and bend round a tin to form circles with a 90mm (3½in) diameter; the ends are wired together to form the eye shapes and are then fixed into position. You now take the

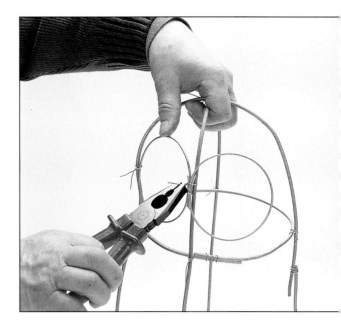

1 Fix the circular eye shapes D in place with fine wire – the combination pliers easily grip and twist the wire to give a secure joint. Wind surplus wire round the frame.

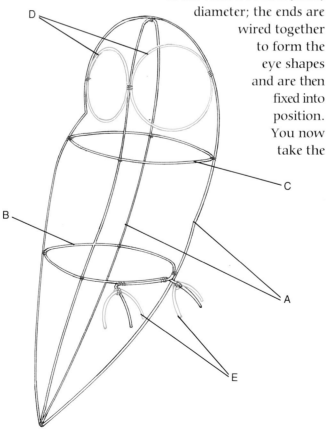

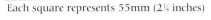
Each square represents 55mm (2¼ inches)

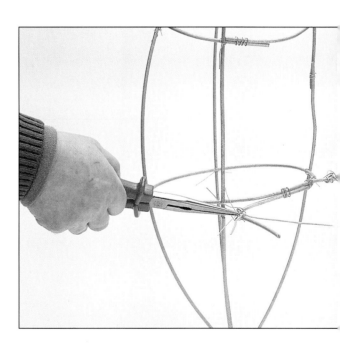

2 Twist E round B to form the owl's claws and then wind fine wire round the joint to secure. Twist the ends with the long-nose pliers to tighten the wire, then wrap surplus wire round the frame.

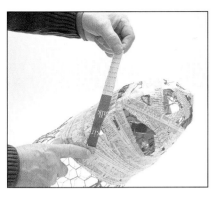

3 Build up the base coat of the papier mâché with strips of paper wound round the framework. Smooth the surface with the fingers to give a smooth finish and good adhesion.

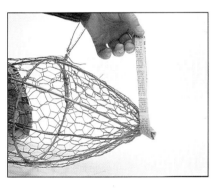

4 Wrap a narrow strip of pasted paper round the tail end and gradually progress towards the head end to join up with areas where the base coat is complete.

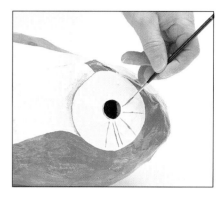

5 Use a filbert shaped hog hair brush to give the feather texture to the owl. Keep the brush fairly dry by wiping off surplus paint, this will give the right impression of plumage.

6 Paint the fine lines round the eye area with a thin pointed sable hair brush. Use your little finger to steady your hand and stop the line wobbling off course.

two E's and wrap round B where the claws have been formed and bend them back on themselves to form the additional claws. These are wired into place and can be moulded to grip the branch or place where it is to be sited.

Take the chicken wire and mould it round the wire frame, securing it into place by twisting loose wire ends round the frame. Surplus wire can be trimmed off to save bulk round the tail and head ends.

Having reached this stage you can start covering the frame with papier mâché, taking care not to make the claws too bulky. Once the papier mâché has been completed and allowed to dry, the whole bird should be treated with the waterproofing solution. The next stage is to prime and paint the owl using suitable colours and using a fine brush for delicate detail, while the suggestion of feathers can be achieved by using a brush with a curved or filbert end with little paint to give a feather texture. Once dry it is now ready to be placed into position where it should be fixed by using the claws to grip. Additional wire can be used to give extra security.

Making a
Papier Mâché
TOUCAN

A flash of bright colour half hidden in green foliage conjures up images of the jungle. You can create this picture in your own garden by making a pair of toucans. Simple to make and easily attached to a branch, each bird will make your garden more interesting, without the raucous noises of the tropics!

40

YOU WILL NEED

4mm wire:
one length 1220mm (48in) (A)
one length 1320mm (52in) (B)

2mm wire:
two lengths 250mm (10in) (C)
one length 200mm (8in) (D)
two lengths 150mm (6in) (E)
one length 405mm (16in) (F)

.9mm wire:
various short lengths for tying the
frame together

chicken wire:
one piece 610 x 230mm (24 x 9in)

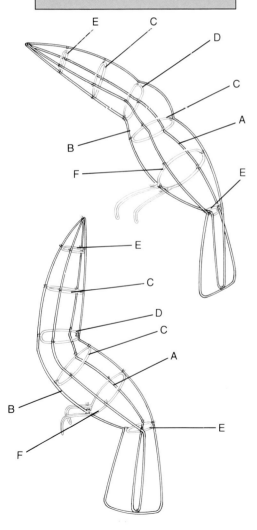

Bend A to form the view of the toucan from above, then use fine wire to secure the overlap of ends. Form B to make the side view of the bird, making sure that it fits with A for size and shape before joining them together with fine wire. Make one C into the cross section of the neck; make sure that it fits round A and B, then wire into place. Bend the other C into the section of the beak that is quite slender, so make a slim oval shape to fit round A and B and fix it in position with wire. Form D into the shape for the join between the head and beak and secure in place to A and B. Make one E into a cross section of the beak close to the tip and wire to A and B. The other E is constructed into the join between the body and tail and secured with wire. Bend F into the cross section of the body with the legs, make sure it fits round A and B, and then tie into place with fine wire. The legs will form the claws and are left to bend round the chosen branch when you have completed the bird.

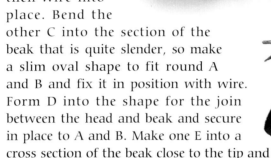

The chicken wire is formed round the framework by squeezing and pulling the mesh out of shape to fit the wire structure. Trim off any excess chicken wire and secure the mesh in place by bending the ends under the adjoining mesh to give a smooth finish. Cover the bird with papier mâché first by winding the strips of pasted paper round the beak like a bandage. Continue with the body, tail and legs until the whole toucan is covered. Build up the layers until the desired thickness is achieved, allow to dry thoroughly before treating with the waterproofing solution. Prime and paint once the surface is dry, keep the colours bright for best effect, and then place in the garden. Bend the claws round the branch to give a firm grip – if the bird is unbalanced, secure the claws in place with small galvanised wire staples. The other toucan follows the same dimensions but you can twist the head to give more variety to the pose.

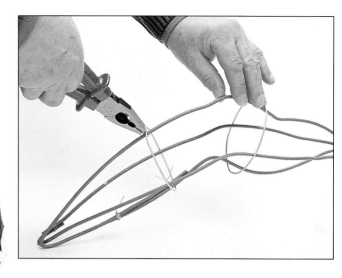

1 Form the oval cross section of the beak with 2mm wire and secure to the main frame with fine wire. Use the combination pliers for a good grip on the wire that gives a strong tight join.

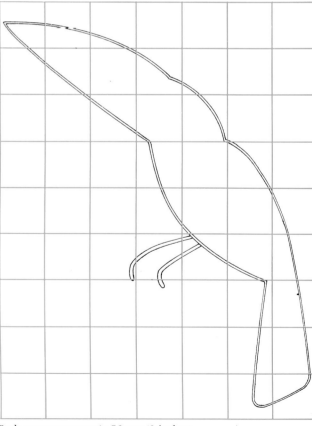

Each square represents 50mm (2 inches)

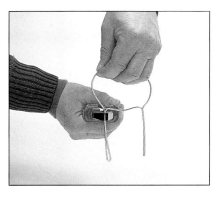

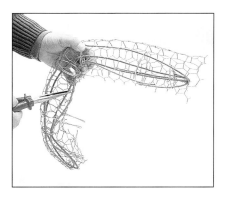

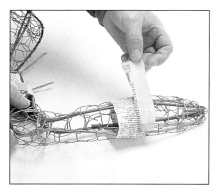

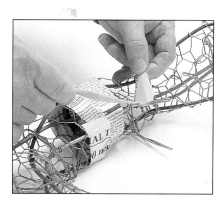

2 Form the length F to make the body and legs. Use the combination pliers to grip the wire while bending it into the sharp angle between the leg and body.

3 Cover the wire framework with chicken wire. Twist the ends under the mesh with long-nose pliers to secure it as you progress towards each end. Trim off surplus wire where necessary.

4 Lay the strips of pasted paper over the beak shape, wrapping them round like a bandage. Work from the centre towards the ends and smooth the surface down with the fingers

5 Wind the paper round the legs. To obtain good adhesion use a modelling tool to hold one end as you pull the other end round. Use the tool to to remove air bubbles.

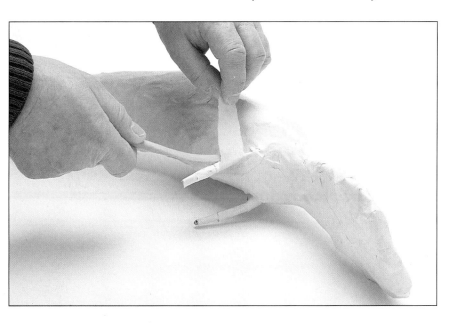

6 The join between the bird's body and leg needs careful modelling to achieve a crisp angle. Use the small end of a modelling tool to rub the papier mâché into tight corners and the broader side to smooth the surface.

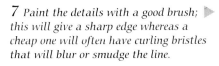

7 Paint the details with a good brush; ▷ this will give a sharp edge whereas a cheap one will often have curling bristles that will blur or smudge the line.

Making a Papier Mâché
WATERLILY

*W*aterlilies are so associated with garden ponds that to imagine one without is like a kilt without a sporran. If you wish to have a permanent waterlily, in and out of season, in bloom and floating in your pond, then this model is for you. Simple in design and easily constructed, the waterlily flower, bud and pads will enhance any stretch of clear water and provide shade and shelter for fish.

You Will Need

2mm wire:
two lengths 685mm (27in) (A)
two lengths 625mm (24½in) (B)
one length 550mm (22in) (C)
one length 510mm (20in) (D)
one length 2335mm (90in) (E)
three lengths 300mm (12in) (F)
one length 250mm (10in) (G)

.9mm wire:
various short lengths to tie the
frame together

chicken wire:
two pieces 230 x 230mm (9 x 9in)
large leaves
two pieces 210 x 210mm
(8¼ x 8¼in) medium leaves
one piece 190 x 190mm
(7½ x 7½in) small leaf

one piece of 25mm (1in) thick
expanded polystyrene or cork 380 x
550mm (15 x 22in) for the float.

Bend one A to make a circle 200mm (8in) in diameter and wire the overlapping ends together. Repeat with the other A: these make the two large leaf shapes. Form the two B's into the medium-sized leaves 75mm (7in) in diameter using the same method. Make the small leaf with C to form a ring 150mm (6in) in diameter. Bend D into the flower base to make a ring 125mm (5in) in diameter. Form E into a flower shape with eight curved petals about 125mm (5in) long. Join D to E with fine wire. Next, make the flower bud, taking two F's and bending them to make the side and front views. Form the remaining F into a circle 75mm (3in) in diameter and wire to the other F's where the frame crosses. Bend G to make a ring 63mm (2½in) in diameter and fix to the two free-ended F's by folding over the wire ends to make loops round G. Pinch the joint tight and wire together.

Cover the leaf shapes with chicken wire by simply laying them in place and folding the edges over the wire rings. Make sure that you bend the sharp wire ends out of the way. Lay the leaves, flower and bud in position and wire together to form the total group.

Apply the papier mâché over the framework, laying strips of pasted paper onto the leaves working from the edges. Wrap paper round the petals, using narrow strips for the petal ends to avoid creases. Leave gaps between the petals to allow water to drain freely. Build up the layers until the required thickness is reached, then apply the water-proofing solution. An additional coat is recommended as the model will be so close to the water level.

1 *Fold the petals from length E, using the combination pliers to give sharp ends to each petal as well as curving them to form a cup shape. Bind the overlap with fine wire.*

Paint with primer, followed by coats of exterior-quality paint and then add details on petals and leaves as needed. Mark out the overall shape of the leaves and flowers on the polystyrene or cork and cut these out with a sharp knife. Prime and spray with a suitable colour: if you are using polystyrene then an aerosol of car-retouching paint will dissolve the surface to give a naturally rough finish. Fit the model to the float and fix with fine wire through the base. You can now launch the completed construction onto the water, either anchoring the group with a weight and nylon line or leaving it free to be blown by the wind over the surface.

2 Place the chicken wire over the wire circle and bend the edges over to form a lily pad. Twist the sharp wire ends out of harm's way with long-nose pliers.

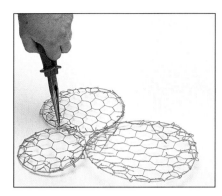

3 Tie the leaves together with fine wire – the long-nose pliers are ideal for reaching in between the chicken wire to twist the joins tight for a secure fixing.

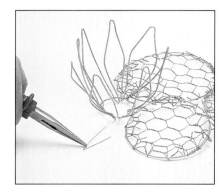

4 Use the long-nose pliers to wire the flower to the lily pads. The narrow points make it easy to insert the fine wire through the netting to make a strong connection.

5 Lay strips of pasted paper over the leaves, folding the ends over the edge and smoothing down with the fingers to provide a good base coat of papier mâché.

6 Use narrow strips of paper to cover the tips of the petals. These are pressed in place using a modelling tool to give good adhesion and a smooth surface.

7 Lay white paper strips over the coloured base coat so that you can see where you have been. Continue with alternate coats to build up the papier mâché to the desired thickness.

8 Colour the flower petals inside and out and add details of veins and markings. Use a fine brush to give crisp lines and sharp edges to the delicate paint work.

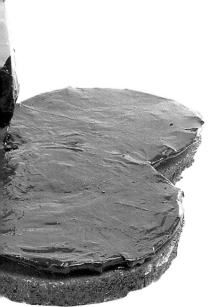

9 Join the float to the plant group with fine wires threaded through the base and secured to the back of the leaves. Note the rough natural edge of the float.

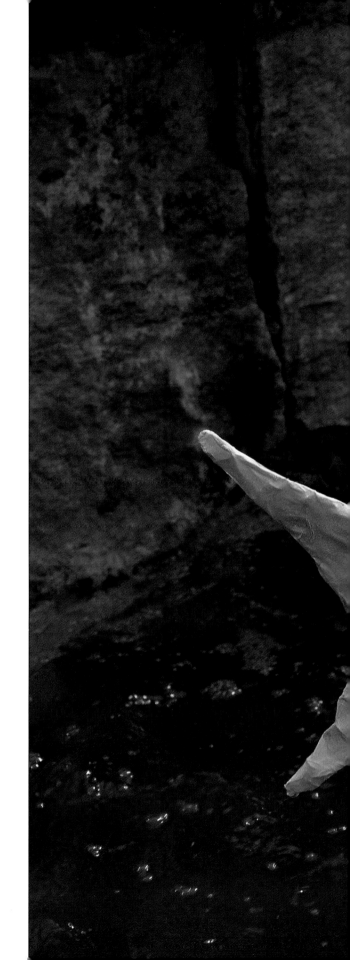

Making a Papier Mâché
LEAPING SALMON

A leaping salmon is a must for anyone who has a waterfall, a real one will not perform to your demands but a papier mâché model will. It is supported on a stout wire that is secured to a concrete base that rests on the floor of the pond. With this model there is no need to explain about 'the one that got away' – it is indisputable evidence of the size of fish in your pond.

48

YOU WILL NEED

4mm wire:
four lengths 1930mm (76in) (A)
one length 710mm (28in) (B)
one length 610mm (24in) (C)
one length 300mm (12in) (D)

2mm wire:
one length 760mm (30in) (E)
three lengths 380mm (15in) (F)
one length 610mm (24in) (G)

.9mm wire:
various short lengths to tie
framework together

chicken wire:
one piece 685 x 610mm (27 x 24in)

B end one A into the side profile of the salmon, remembering that it is curved both vertically and laterally to give it life. Bind the overlap with fine wire. Form another A into the plan view of the fish, checking that the curves fit to the side profile exactly, and then wire together at nose and tail. Make the remaining two A's into the stand, forming a circular base at one end and a cross section of the fish at the other. Bind these two A's with fine wire along their lengths. Insert the cross section into the fish shape and wire all the A's together, making sure that you give the structure good balance. Bend B into a cross section of the fish to fit behind the support, then secure it in place with fine wire. Form C into a cross section behind the head and fix it in place. Make D into a cross

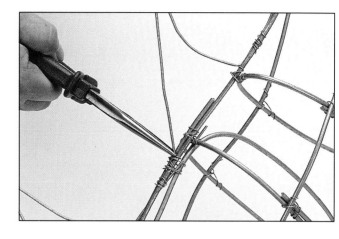

1 Join the fins onto the main frame with fine wire. Wind the wire round the frame and squeeze tight with long-nose pliers to provide a strong structure.

2 Fold the chicken wire over the tail fins and squeeze the mesh flat with the pliers. This gives a crisp edge. Make sure all the sharp wire ends are bent out of harm's way.

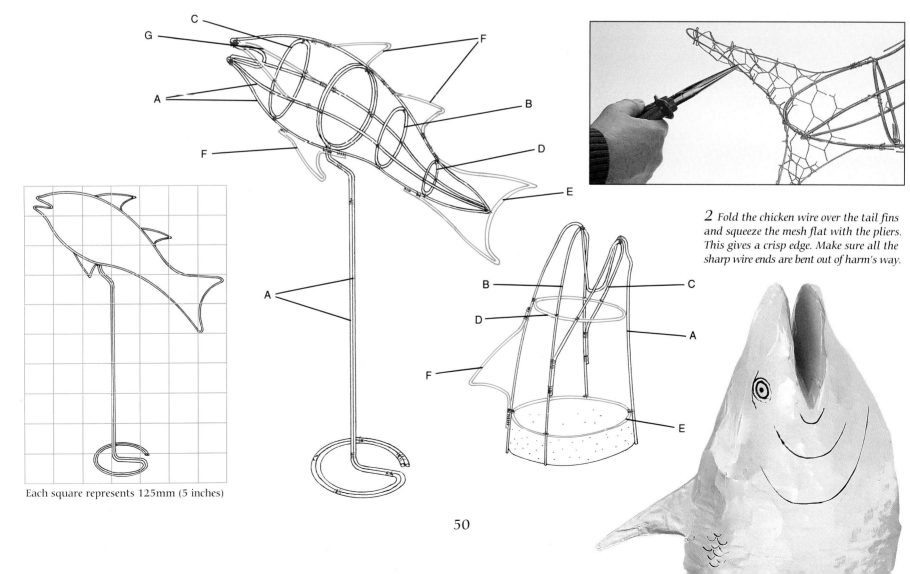

Each square represents 125mm (5 inches)

50

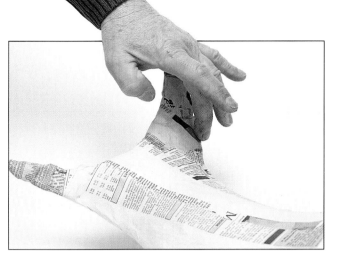

3 Cover the coloured base coat with a layer of white pasted paper to show you where you have already been, smoothing the surface with the fingers to give a good finish.

4 Use small pieces of pasted paper to cover small curves and difficult areas. Press the paper in place with a modelling tool to give a fine finish and good adhesion.

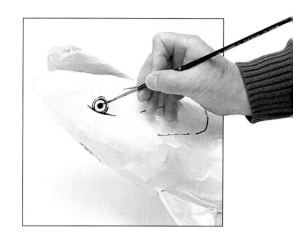

5 Make the fish-scale texture with a filbert-shaped brush. Keep the bristles fairly dry of paint so the base coat will show through the brush strokes and give the desired effect.

section near the tail and wire it together where the frame crosses. Bend E into the tail fin and wire it in position. Form the three F's into fin shapes and secure in place to the back spine and underbelly with fine wire. Make G into the upper jaw of the mouth and wire it to the side frame of the fish.

Cover the frame with chicken wire, moulding it by squeezing and pulling the mesh into shape, then trim off surplus and secure in place by bending over the wire edges through the adjacent netting.

Lay strips of pasted paper over the completed framework to form the base coat of papier mâché. Continue until you reach the required thickness and allow to dry. Treat the surface with waterproofing solution and follow the manufacturer's instructions exactly as the model will be in close contact with water.

Suspend the model 25mm (1in) above a smooth non-porous surface and pack moist concrete around the wire base until you have at least 25mm (1in) of concrete above the frame and extending to 180mm (7in) radius round the support. When this is dry, treat it with a pond paint to stop alkaline

salts from seeping into the water.

Prime the surface of the papier mâché and decorate it with exterior quality paint. Use a fine brush to detail the scales and spray some silver over the top to give a sheen to the surface. Place in the pool near the waterfall with the fish above the water level. Take care if the pool has a liner – place some packing under the concrete base to prevent the liner from damage. Where the water is deep build up a base with blocks to achieve the correct level.

6 Draw in the details of the eye, gills and scales with a fine pointed brush. This gives a clean sharp line and crisp edges to the paintwork. Keep the hand steady while working.

Making a
Papier Mâché
TOTEM POLE

*R*ed Indians loved to decorate their camps with totem poles – upright tree trunks richly carved and coloured with emblems of their tribe.
A vertical collection of heads, eagles, animals, serpents and mystical beings makes an exciting feature in a garden. If you can manage to stop the pole being used in the children's play area it is an original object as a focal point. Placed in the front garden it will make your home distinctly unique.

Bend one A into the side profile of the totem pole – you will need plenty of space in which to wield this length of wire safely. Form the other A into the front view, check that its measurements match to the first A. Make B's into cross sections of the pole and then join A's and B's together with fine wire. It is wise to cross brace the framework with H's as you progress to keep the structure rigid. Place each H diagonally up the framework and bend the ends over the mainframe where the wires cross, pinch them tight and then tie with wire. Continue to make the cross sections from C's, D's, E's, F's and G, then place these in position and secure with wire.

Cover the framework with chicken wire, starting at the top and moulding the netting to fit tight to the frame. Work towards the base and finally fold the mesh over wire B to give a neat finish to the pole. This will leave lengths of the A's protruding. Bend these at right angles at least 25mm (1in) below B to form anchors to be set in the concrete base later.

Stick strips of paper over the framework to build up a covering of papier mâché. Use alternate coats of coloured and white paper to monitor the number of layers. When you reach the required thickness, allow to dry and then spray the interior and exterior with water-proofing solution. Follow the manufacturer's directions for best results.

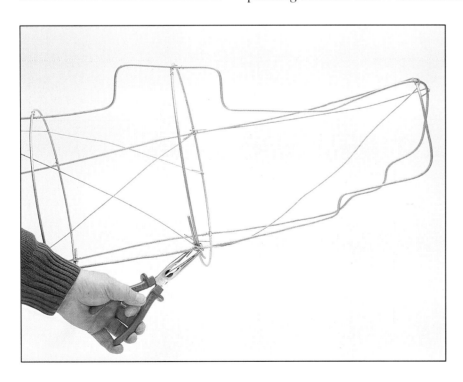

1 Fix cross braces to keep the framework rigid, using the long-nose pliers to bend the ends over to anchor the braces to the main frame. Secure with fine wire.

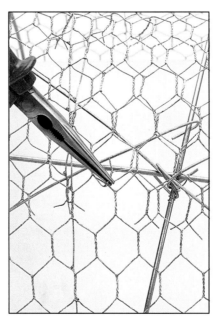

2 Fold over the sharp wire ends behind the adjacent chicken wire with the long-nose pliers. Then squeeze to secure the netting in position and form the base for the papier mâché.

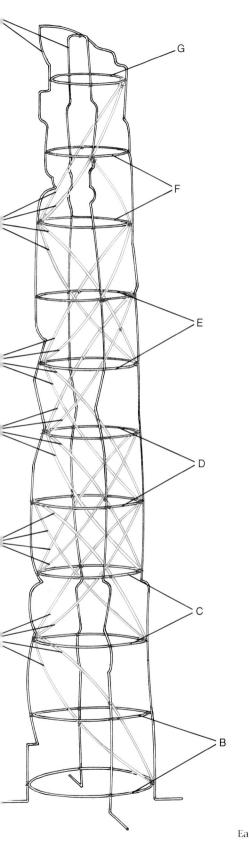

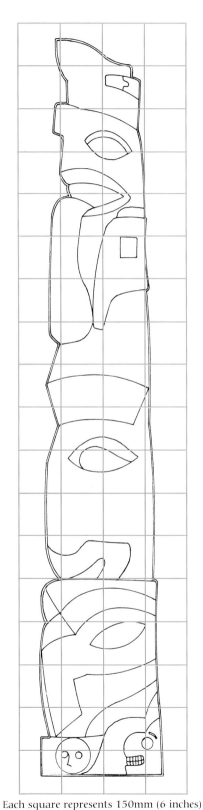

Each square represents 150mm (6 inches)

3 Lay strips of pasted paper along the bottom of the totem pole. Use the cut edge of the torn newspaper to give a clean finish to the base edge, rather than the rough side.

4 Draw the black lines and details of the eye with a fine pointed brush.

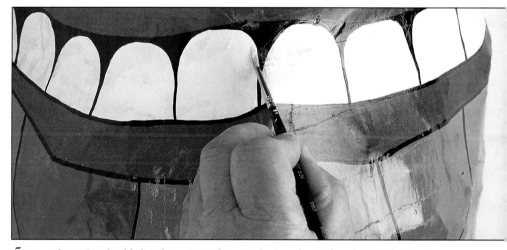

5 Use a fine pointed sable brush to give a sharp and crisp edge to the white teeth. Steady the hand with the little finger to provide a smooth finish to the line.

Prime the surface and mark out the markings and shapes with pencil. Now use exterior quality paint to colour the totem pole. Set the anchor wires into a slab of moist concrete to allow at least 25mm (1in) of concrete to be above and below the wires and to extend to at least 150mm (6in) beyond the perimeter of the base. Check that the pole is vertical and allow it to dry for two or three days. You can now move it into its garden setting and if anyone says "How", you can hand them these instructions...

Making
Papier Mâché
SWANS

A pair of swans resting on the pool surface provides great interest, especially where there is a dark shady area. They have a complex body shape with a slender neck that you can easily make out of wire and mesh. To make them float you will need to construct a simple platform of cork or expanded polystyrene. You will find that by making a pair of swans and securing them to a single large float they will become far more stable than one alone.

YOU WILL NEED

ONE SWAN
(approximate measurements):

4mm wire:
one length 3200mm (126in) (A)
one length 3350mm (132in) (B)
one length 1955mm (77in) (C)
two lengths 1270mm (50in) (D)
two lengths 870mm (34in) (E)

2mm wire:
three lengths 230mm (9in) (F)
two lengths 300mm (12in) (G)
.9mm wire: various short lengths
for tying the frame together

chicken wire:
one piece 915 x 230mm
(36 x 9in) for head and neck
one piece 230 x 250mm (9 x 10in)
for base of neck
one piece 915 x 1220mm
(36 x 48in) for body

**25mm (1in) expanded
polystyrene or cork:**
one piece 610mm x 1220mm
(24 x 48in) to take two swans,
one piece 610mm (24in) square
should support one swan. These
dimensions could vary depending
on the quantity of papier mâché
used: the thicker the covering, the
heavier it will be and you will
then need either a larger surface
area or a thicker piece of
buoyancy material.

Take A and bend into shape to form the side view of the swan. When the outline is satisfactory, bind the two ends together with fine wire. Next take B and form the plan view of the bird, checking with the dimensions of A before binding the ends together. C is then formed following the diagram, also checking that it fits with A and B. You then join them together using the fine wire where the frame wire crosses. Take one D and bend it into shape to form the flat base to the swan, it is then wired into position. The other D is moulded into shape to form the cross section of the body and then secured into place with wire. You now take both E's and form them to make cross sections of the tail and breast of the bird. Secure them into place. The F's and G's are curved to form the neck and head sections and wired into their positions.

Once you have completed the framework of wire you prepare the chicken wire covering. Start with the neck and head as these are simple forms. Carefully mould the mesh to form a smooth natural shape round the framework twisting the wire ends round the thicker wires to give a flush surface with no sharp ends protruding. This is followed with the base of the neck and finally the larger piece for the body. The latter is moulded to form the wings as well as the body. Take time to smooth out kinks and folds to provide a good surface to take the papier mâché – extra

time that you spend at this stage will save much time later trying to remedy ugly forms. Once the metal framework is completed the papier mâché is applied in layers to cover the surface. When sufficient layers are completed and allowed to dry the model is then waterproofed. Additional treatment around the lower edge could be advisable due to its proximity to the water. The interior is sprayed with the treatment to ensure that you reach the papier mâché hidden behind the chicken wire.

Once the model is dried thoroughly a coat of primer is applied and is then followed with coats of exterior paint to give the appearance of a swan. If the floating platform is expanded polystyrene use a coat of a darkish coloured paint (a car-retouching aerosol is ideal) to camouflage the white colour. The paint will partially dissolve the surface and edges, giving an irregular but natural finish. You then wire the swans to the platform with them preferably facing in opposite directions to provide a good balance. If the swans are particularly heavy and the board does not give adequate floatation, an extra piece can be added underneath. Take the wire through holes made in the platform to give a secure fixing.

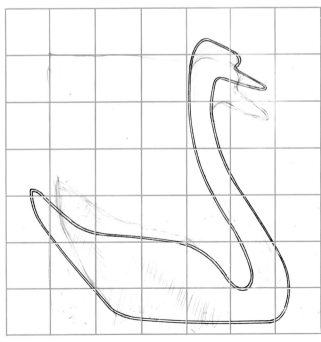

Each square represents 125mm (5 inches)

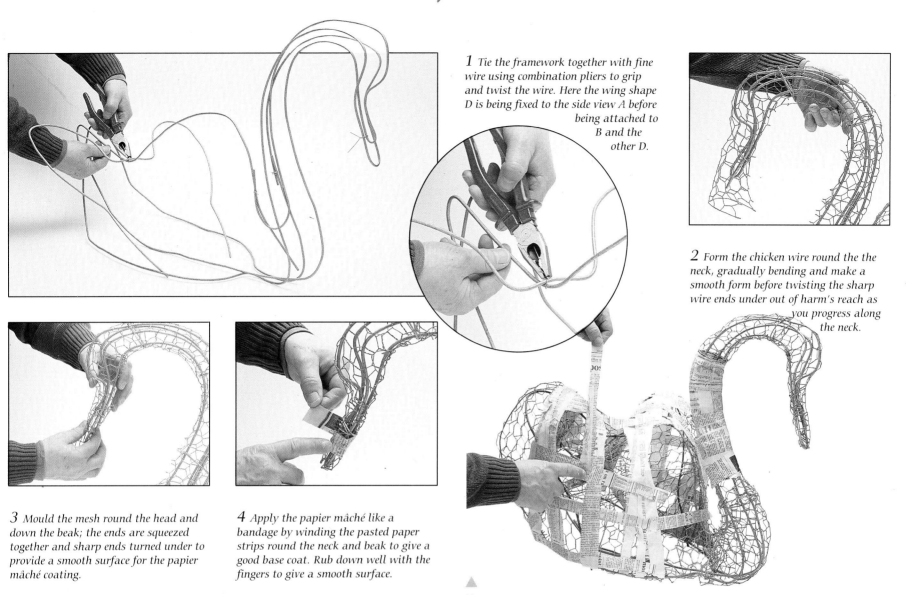

1 Tie the framework together with fine wire using combination pliers to grip and twist the wire. Here the wing shape D is being fixed to the side view A before being attached to B and the other D.

2 Form the chicken wire round the the neck, gradually bending and make a smooth form before twisting the sharp wire ends under out of harm's reach as you progress along the neck.

3 Mould the mesh round the head and down the beak; the ends are squeezed together and sharp ends turned under to provide a smooth surface for the papier mâché coating.

4 Apply the papier mâché like a bandage by winding the pasted paper strips round the neck and beak to give a good base coat. Rub down well with the fingers to give a smooth surface.

5 As there is little surface to stick to it is best to make an initial lattice of strips and gradually infill the gaps. This is particularly important with large areas where there is little shape to grip.

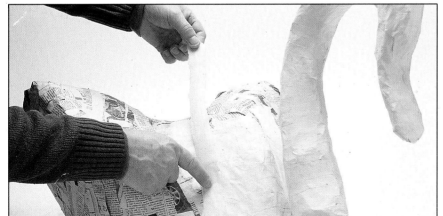

6 Lay additional coats over the base and rub down to give good adhesion and provide a good surface. Continue pasting on the layers until you reach the required thickness.

7 Paint the finer details after the larger areas have been covered and dried, use a small pointed brush for crisp details and steady the hand by using the little finger as a support.

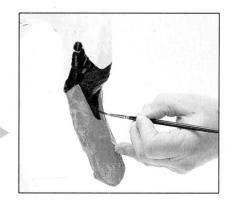

Making a
Papier Mâché
PANDA

Of all the different bears available the panda has the most distinctive markings, its black and white livery is dramatic and very decorative, making it easily recognisable. To have your own tame panda without the drawbacks of feeding it on fresh bamboo shoots and restricting its movements is easily achieved. A papier mâché model allows you to have the enjoyment of a panda and to move it round the garden at will.

YOU WILL NEED

4mm wire:
one length 2440mm (96in) (A)
one length 2285mm (90in) (B)
one length 510mm (20in) (C)
one length 1830mm (72in) (D)
three lengths 2030mm (80in) (E)
two lengths 815mm (33in) (F)
one length 1675mm (66in) (G)
one length 1525mm (60in) (H)
three lengths 1015mm (40in) (I)

2mm wire:
one length 665mm (26in) (J)
one length 735mm (29in) (K)
two lengths 510mm (20in) (L)

.9mm wire:
various short lengths to tie
framework together

chicken wire:
one piece 915 x 815mm
(36 x 32in) back
one piece 870 x 710mm
(34 x 28in) head
one piece 870 x 455mm
(34 x 18in) front
two pieces 455 x 300mm
(18 x 12in) arms

Make A into side view of the body and head, bind the overlap with fine wire. Bend B into the back shape and feet then wire to A. Form C into the back link that fits to B and wire to A and B to make the base of the back. Make D into the cross section of the lower body and thighs then secure to A and B. Bend two E's into side views of the panda's body from shoulder to bottom and wire to B, C and D. Make the remaining E into the front view of the chest and arms then fix to A with fine wire. Form both F's into side views of the leg profiles and wire to B and D. Make G into the cross section of the chest and fix to A and E's. Bend H into the top view of the head with ears and secure to A at back and nose with fine wire. Form the three I's into sections of the head and join to A and H where the frame crosses. Make J into the hook shape of the arm and secure to E's and G. Bend K into the other arm and fix to E's and G with fine wire. Form the two L's into cross sections of the arms and wire in place to E, J and K.

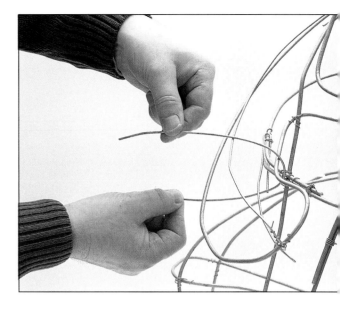

1 *Bend the arm cross section into position and secure with fine wire where the frame crosses. Twist the wire tight and wind the surplus round the frame.*

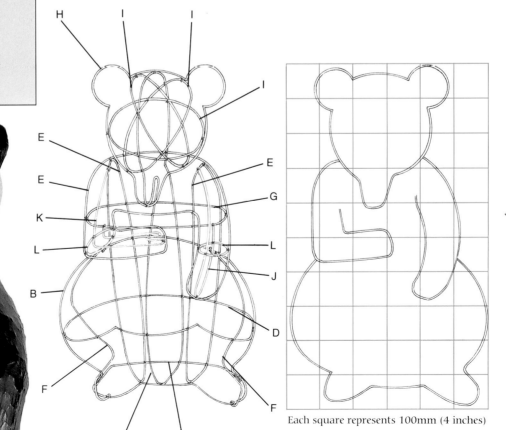

Each square represents 100mm (4 inches)

2 *The completed framework is now ready to be covered with the chicken wire. Make sure that you twist tight all joins with the pliers and that no sharp wire ends left exposed.*

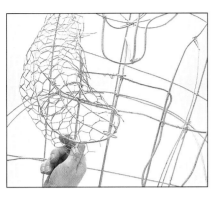

3 Place the partially formed chicken wire round the arm, trim off surplus mesh and fix in place to the frame. Bend over the sharp wire ends out of harm's way.

4 Use a modelling tool to push strips of pasted paper into the groove for gripping a piece of bamboo. Smooth over the ends to leave the surface free from creases.

5 The papier mâché surface is built up and sharp internal angles are made crisp by using a bone folder: the point will reach into small crevices and the side will smooth larger areas.

6 Use a fine pointed brush to give a clean crisp edge to the areas of paint round the ears. To steady the hand when painting detail use the little finger as a rest.

7 Paint the eye detail with a fine pointed brush to give a clean edge to the area. If the paint is thick and sticky dilute it with a little turps to make it flow freely.

Cover the framework with chicken wire, beginning with the large simple shapes and working towards the more complicated forms. Make a groove in the end of one arm to act as a paw to grip a piece of bamboo if required. Secure the netting in place by folding the wire edges round the frame and into the adjacent mesh. Trim off the surplus chicken wire and use to fill odd gaps in the covering.

Lay strips of pasted paper over the completed framework, form a lattice of strips to support the base coat of papier mâché. Continue to build up sufficient thickness using alternate colour and white layers. Allow to dry thoroughly before applying the waterproofing solution, follow the manufacturer's instructions for best results.

Prime the papier mâché surface and decorate the panda with exterior quality paint in black and white. You can now put the panda in your garden in the place of your choice either as a striking focal point or as a surprise among shrubs.

Making a
Papier Mâché
TEDDY BEAR
& FLOWERPOT

*A*dd something special to
your garden. Most of us
gardeners have containers with
floral displays of one kind or
another but it is rare to have
something unique. Choose
a container with a hint of
the honeypot about it and
then construct a teddy-bear
to embrace it. In order to
make the bear fit your flowerpot you will have
to adjust the measurements and angles for the
two to fit comfortably together.

YOU WILL NEED

4mm wire:
two lengths 1625mm (64in) (A)
two lengths 1650mm (65in) (B)
one length 1700mm (67in) (C)
one length 2030mm (80in) (D)
one length 915mm (36in) (E)
two lengths 760mm (30in) (F)

2mm wire:
four lengths 250mm (10in) (G)
three lengths 330mm (13in) (H)
two lengths 455mm (18in) (I)

.9mm wire:
various short lengths to tie the
framework together

chicken wire:
one piece 455 x 455mm
(18 x 18in) back
one piece 405 x 300mm
(16 x 12in) front
two pieces 355 x 355mm
(14 x 14in) legs
two pieces 355 x 250mm
(14 x 10in) arms
one piece 915 x 710mm
(36 x 28in) head

Bend one A into the side profile of the body and head and bind the overlap together with fine wire. Form the other A into the front view of the body and head and join both A's together at the head and bottom. Make one B into the front view of the arms with the top wire going behind the neck and the lower wire moulded round the chest. Bend the other B into the plan view of the arms and chest. Fix both B's in position to A's and secure with fine wire. Form C into the plan view of the legs and body and join to A's. Make D into the front profile of the legs and feet, then wire to A's and C. Bend E into the plan view of the head and nose then secure in place to A's. Form F's into vertical cross sections of the head and join to A's and E with fine wire. Make the G's into cross sections of the arms then secure to B's. Bend two H's into cross sections of the legs and wire in position to C and D. Form the other H into a cross section of the nose then join to A and E. Make I's into profiles of the soles of the feet and wire to C and D. Check that the bear fits comfortably round the flowerpot – adjust if necessary at this stage by bending the arms and legs.

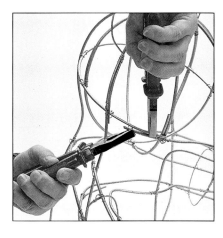

1 *Adjust the curve of the wire with two pairs of combination pliers. These will give excellent grip and will bend the wire with little effort.*

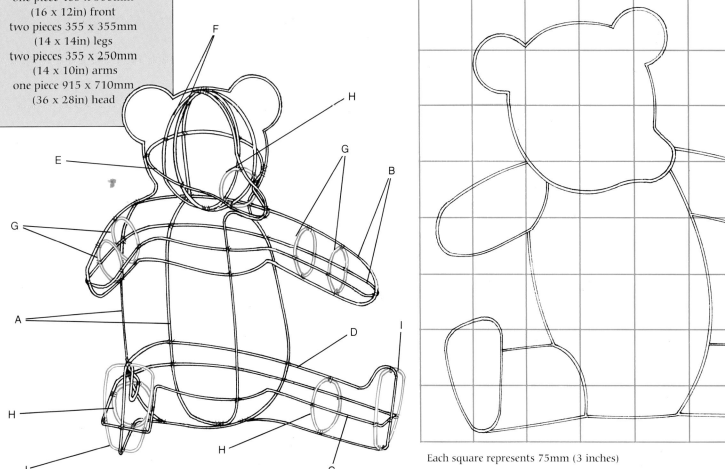

Each square represents 75mm (3 inches)

Cover the framework with chicken wire: start with the simple areas like the back and work towards those that have a deal of moulding and shaping. Anchor the mesh and turn under all sharp wire ends out of harm's way.

Lay strips of pasted paper over the framework to form the base coat of papier mâché. Continue to build up the layers until you reach the required thickness. Allow to dry thoroughly and then treat the surface with waterproofing solution. Follow the manufacturer's instructions carefully.

Prime the surface and decorate the bear with exterior quality paint. You can now position the bear slightly to one side of the container so that it can peer round the planting rather than be hidden behind the display.

2 Undertake the finer modelling with the fingers, squeezing and pulling the mesh into place.

3 Use narrow strips of pasted paper to wrap round the tight curves and small forms such as the nose. Rub well down to give good adhesion and a smooth surface.

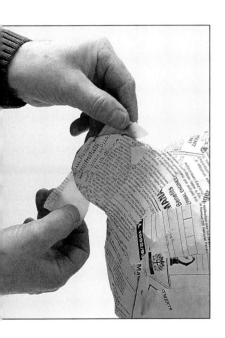

4 Stick short strips of paper round the ears; this allows some paper to fold over the edge. Repeat this method on the other side of the ear to give complete coverage.

5 Draw in the edges with a fine pointed brush to give a crisp ▶ finish. Dilute the paint with a little turps if it is a bit thick and sticky to allow a free clear line.

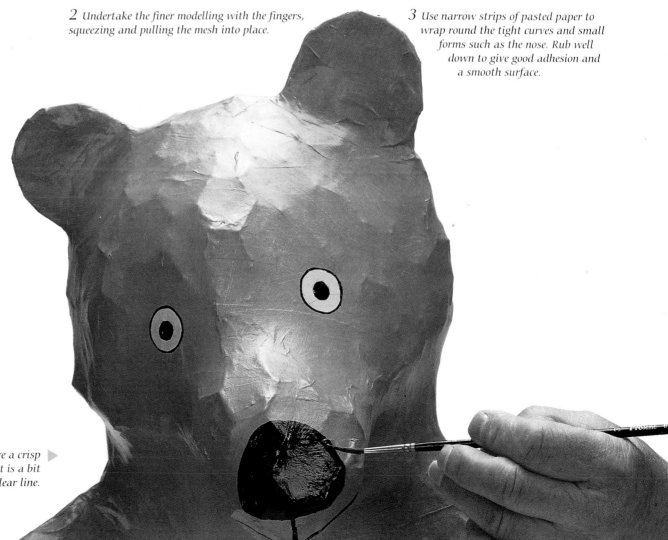

GRIZZLY BEAR

*F*or some a life-sized grizzly bear is more than
a little awe-inspiring – in fact it can be
overbearing, striking a chord of fear when met.
Yet knowing that this beast relies solely on its
bulky presence to make you hesitate does
provide a degree of security. The shadowy form
of this grizzly on a dark night will deter
unwanted visitors from wandering round the
garden. In daylight this bear is a great
favourite with the children who soon come to
terms with the gentle giant. The bear can be set
in a concrete base as a permanent feature or
else its anchor wires can be left straight to act
as spikes to be sunk into the ground. It is then
easily moved from site to site.

YOU WILL NEED

4mm wire:
one length 5485mm (216in) (A)
two lengths 3660mm (144in) (B)
two lengths 3050mm (120in) (C)
one length 2285mm (90in) (D)
one length 2135mm (84in) (E)
two lengths 1980mm (78in) (F)
four lengths 1830mm (72in) (G)
one length 915mm (36in) (H)
four lengths 1065mm (42in) (I)
three lengths 1575mm (62in) (J)
one length 1170mm (46in) (K)
one length 510mm (20in) (L)
one length 710mm (28in) (M)

2mm wire:
two lengths 610mm (24in) (N)
four lengths 510mm (20in) (O)
two lengths 1015mm (40in) (P)

.9mm wire:
various short lengths to tie frame
together

chicken wire:
one piece 915 x 2030mm
(36 x 80in) lower body
one piece 760 x 455mm
(30 x 18in) back
one piece 685 x 455mm
(27 x 18in) front
two pieces 915 x 380mm
(36 x 15in) legs
one piece 915 x 760mm
(36 x 30in) head
two pieces 815 x 610mm
(32 x 24in) arms

Bend A to form the front view of the grizzly without ears and arms and bind the overlap together with fine wire. Make B's into side views of the body and legs. Leave the ends at the feet free at this point, keeping them straight if they are to be used as spikes inserted into the ground, or bent at right angles 25mm (1in) below the base of the foot if the bear is going to be set into concrete. Wire B's to A. Form C's to be side views of the body without the head or feet and then fix in place with fine wire to A and B's. Bend D into the cross section of the lower body and top of the legs and wire to A, B's and C's. Make E into the bear's 'waist' cross section and secure to A, B's and C's with fine wire.

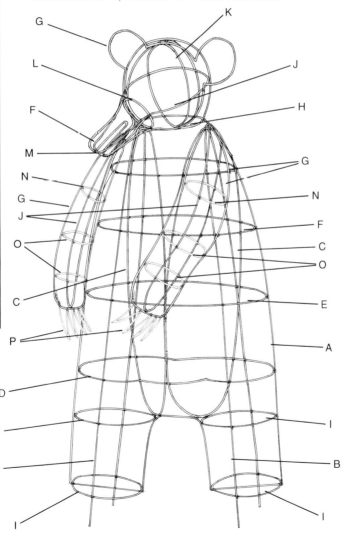

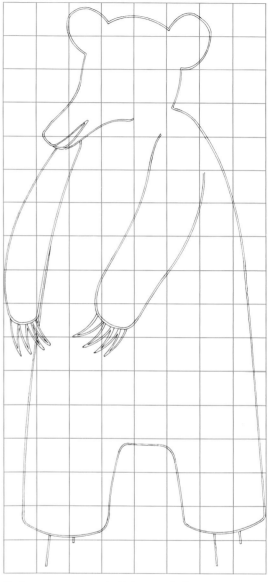

Each square represents 125mm (5 inches)

1 Use the combination pliers to bend the wire into groups of four claws. First form the zig-zag and then curve each spur individually to form a natural-looking claw.

Form one F into the cross section of the chest and join to A, B's and C's. Bend the other F into the side view of the head and fix in position to A. Make one G into the cross section of the upper chest and secure in place with fine wire to A, B's and C's. Take another G and mould into the front view of the head with ears, wire to F. Make the remaining two G's into side views of the arms but keep apart from the body. Form H into the neck section and join to A, F and G. Bend the four I's into cross sections of the legs and feet, join to A and B's with fine wire. Form two of the J's into front views of the arms and keep with the two G's for the moment. The remaining J is made into the plan view of the head and is wired to A, F, G and H. Make K into the front view of the head at eye level and secure in place to F and J. Similarly make L into a cross section of the nose before the mouth starts and wire into position. Bend M into a plan view of the lower

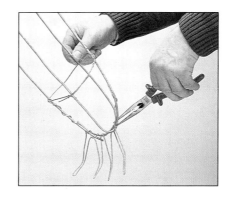

2 Join the claw onto the end of the arm by twisting the surplus wire round the framework and anchor each spur to the frame with fine wire using the long-nose pliers.

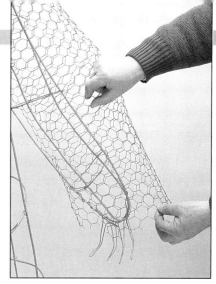

3 Half form the chicken wire before placing on the framework of the arm, then mould the mesh to fit the frame exactly by squeezing and pulling the netting.

4 Cover the claws with strips of pasted paper, tearing these to length and winding them round the metal frame. Firm them with the finger and turn the edge over to give a smooth finish.

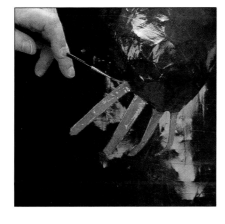

5 Use a fine brush to paint the claws, the point will reach into the corners and crevices between each claw to give a good coating of paint.

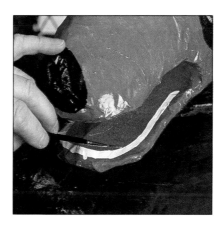

6 Paint the interior of the mouth red and then colour the line of teeth as a long strip of white. This method provides an effective impression of teeth from a distance.

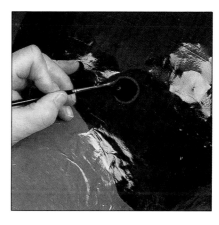

7 For a slightly sinister effect paint a red line round the eye with a fine pointed brush; this is less dramatic than a white line but it makes the bear's appearance more awe-inspiring.

jaw, check that it fits to the upper jaw and join to F and J with fine wire. Form the N's into cross sections of the upper arms and wire to the G's and J's that you have kept separate. Also take the four O's and make into cross sections of the lower arms and join to G's and J's to form the whole arm framework. They are now positioned and secured to A with fine wire. Bend the two P's into claws and fix to G's and J's.

Cover the completed framework with chicken wire. Use the large pieces first and fix them in place, trimming off the excess mesh and keeping this to cover the ears. Continue to mould each piece of netting and secure it to the framework until you have covered the whole. Bend

over all the wire ends, threading them through the adjacent mesh to keep them out of the way.

Form the base coat of papier mâché with strips of pasted paper. With this size model use wide strips of paper to cover the broad areas quickly and then build up the layers until the required thickness is reached. Allow to dry thoroughly before spraying the outside and the inside with waterproofing solution.

Prime the surface and decorate with exterior quality paint to create the grizzly's livery. You can now set it into concrete if you wish, or leave the spikes straight to sink into the soil.

Making a
Papier Mâché
DRAGON

*Y*ou don't have to be a Welshman to want your own personal dragon, anyone can make and enjoy their pet monster. You can place the dragon in a prominent position elevated on a plinth or set among the vegetables as a bird scarer, but however it is displayed it will receive plenty of attention. This dragon is guaranteed not to molest young maidens, burn crops, upset the cattle or breathe fire at Saint George.

72

You Will Need

4mm wire:
two lengths 7315mm (288in) (A)
five lengths 915mm (36in) (B)
four lengths 665mm (26in) (C)
six lengths 380mm (15in) (D)
one length 355mm (14in) (E)
one length 300mm (12in) (F)
two lengths 250mm (10in) (G)
two lengths 1525mm (60in) (H)
two lengths 1625mm (64in) (I)
two lengths 2030mm (80in) (J)
two lengths 1930mm (76in) (K)
two lengths 685mm (27in) (L)
two lengths 3050mm (120in) (M)
two lengths 1370mm (54in) (N)
two lengths 2135mm (84in) (O)

2mm wire:
one length 4060mm (160in) (P)
two lengths 1420mm (56in) (Q)
one length 1015mm (40in) (R)

.9mm wire:
various short lengths to tie the
framework together

chicken wire:
one piece 915 c 510mm
(36 x 20in) tail
two pieces 915 x 915mm
(36 x 36in) body and neck
two pieces 380 x 380mm
(15 x 15in) jaws
four pieces 510 x 380mm
(20 x 15in) legs

Bend one A into the side profile of the dragon, making sure that you have plenty of room to wield this length of wire around as you bend it. Bind the overlap with fine wire. Form the other A into the plan view. Make sure that you form it with curves to give it animation and also that both A's fit together before securing at nose and tail. Form one B into the lower jaw and then fix it to A's. Bend the other four B's into cross sections of the body and wire to A's. Form the four C's into cross sections of the neck and head, then join to A's with wire. Make two D's into sections of the upper jaw and secure to A's. Bend two D's, E, F and G's into cross sections of the tail, then wire to A's. Form H's into side profiles of the front legs then mould them round A's and adjacent cross sections before wiring them together where the frame crosses.

Make I's into side views of the back legs and similarly join to A's. Bend J into the front view of the back legs, then secure to A's and I's with fine wire where the frame crosses. Form K into the front view of the front legs and fix in place to A's and H's. Make L's into cross sections of the thighs on the back legs and join to I's and J. Mould the two D's into cross sections of the front legs, then place them in position and fix to H's and K's. Bend M into the two wings with support under the body. Secure in place with fine wire. Form N's into wing supports to run along the A's

1 Join the wire edge of the wing to the support with fine wire, bind it tightly round and squeeze the wire ends with the long-nose pliers to make a firm joint.

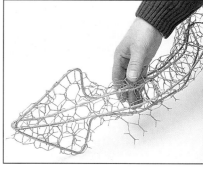

2 Cover the tail section with chicken wire, moulding it carefully with the fingers to follow the shape of the wire frame. Tuck in all loose wire ends out of harm's way.

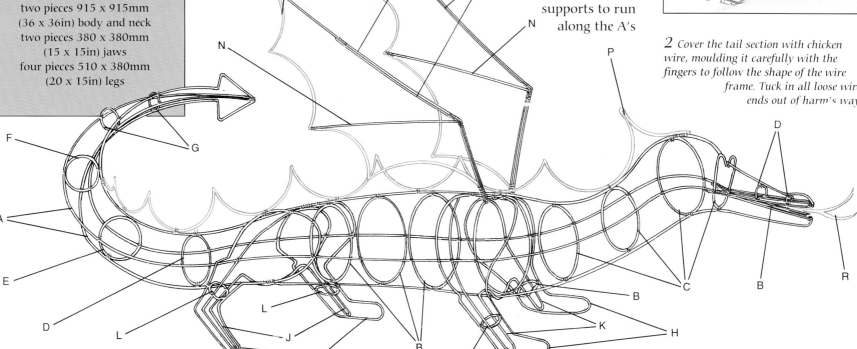

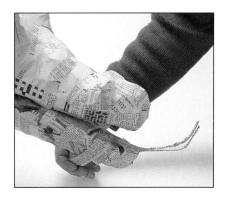

3 Use large strips of pasted paper to build up the wings. Lay them in place overlapping the previous strip, then fold the ends over the edge to stick to the back.

4 Continue to build up the wing with strips of paper. Cover any exposed pasted areas on the back with pieces of paper to leave a smooth and clean surface.

5 Stick strips of paper round the lower jaw to cover the inside of the mouth, then firm down with the fingers to give a smooth surface without creases.

6 Bind strips of pasted paper round the upper jaw to cover the roof of the mouth. Use narrow strips when covering the forms of the nostrils to avoid wrinkles.

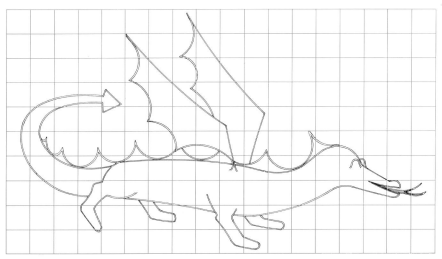

Each square represents 150mm (6 inches)

up M to the angle and drop down to support the wing edge. Make O's into the same shapes as M but shorter on the wings. Bind M, N's and O's together where they run side by side with fine wire. Bend P to form the spikes along the spine and then secure to A. Form the two Q's into the fluted wing edge, then join them to M, N's and O's. Make R into the forked tongue, then fix it to A and B with fine wire.

Cover the framework with chicken wire, but leave the wings and back spines uncovered. Start with the simple pieces without much modelling, then progress to the more complicated forms until it is completed. Trim off surplus mesh and keep it for filling gaps around the feet and legs.

Lay strips of pasted paper over the framework and gradually build up to the required thickness. The spines and wings have no mesh support so take care when covering these areas. Do not make the covering on the wings too thick as the weight could bend the wing supports. Four layers are sufficient, but remember they will be vulnerable to piercing. Allow the papier mâché to dry thoroughly and then apply the waterproofing liquid. Follow the manufacturer's instructions for best results.

Prime the surface and decorate with exterior quality paint. You can now position the dragon in your garden. You will probably find it easier to have two people to carry it, especially through confined spaces like doors, as the wings have quite a spread. If you wish to place it in an exposed position you will need to tether the feet securely. Bind the feet with nylon cord tied to stakes driven into the ground to prevent the dragon from being blown over.

7 Paint the inside of the mouth with a contrasting colour to the skin, and then use a white line to suggest the teeth. A fine pointed brush is ideal for painting this line.

8 Use a good quality hog hair brush to suggest the dragon's scaly skin. Use a darker paint than the body colour.

Making a
Papier Mâché
GIRAFFE

*O*ne hesitates to have a full-sized giraffe in the garden, its height alone will make it stand out head and neck above the average garden growth. By scaling down the model and making a young giraffe, the size will fit into the ordinary garden and still make a spectacular point of interest. Its decorative spotted coat and unusual shape help to focus attention on it.

76

YOU WILL NEED

4mm wire:
two lengths 4060mm (160in) (A)
one length 5485mm (216in) (B)
one length 4570mm (180in) (C)
four lengths 2795mm (110in) (D)
one length 1270mm (50in) (E)
one length 915mm (36in) (F)
two lengths 1015mm (40in) (G)
one length 815mm (32in) (H)
one length 550mm (22in) (I)
one length 455mm (18in) (J)
one length 355mm (14in) (K)
one length 1830mm (72in) (L)

2mm wire:
two lengths 610mm (24in) (M)
two lengths 510mm (20in) (N)
two lengths 380mm (15in) (O)
four lengths 355mm (14in) (P)
four lengths 300mm (12in) (Q)
four lengths 265mm (10 ½in) (R)
four lengths 230mm (9in) (S)
one length 1015mm (40in) (T)
two lengths 200mm (8in) (U)

.9mm wire:
various short lengths to tie the
framework together

chicken wire:
one piece 915 x 915mm
(36in) neck
one piece 915 x 1015mm
(36 x 40in) body
one piece 355 x 455mm
(14 x 18in) head
two pieces 915 x 530mm
(36 x 21in) front legs
two pieces 610 x 355mm
(24 x 14in) back legs
one piece 550 x 125mm
(22 x 5in) tail

Bend one A into the side view of the head, neck and body, then bind the overlap with fine wire. Form the other A into the plan view of the head, neck and body, checking that it fits to the first A exactly. Make B into the front view of the forelegs and wire A's and B together where the frame crosses. Keep the legs splayed to give the giraffe stability. Bend C into the front view of the back legs and join to A's and B with fine wire. Form two D's into side views of the front legs and join to A's and B. Make the other two D's into side views of the back legs and fix to A's and C where the framework crosses. Bend E into the cross section of the body by the front legs and wire in place to A's, B and D's. Form F into a cross section of the body near the back legs and secure in position to A's, C and D's. Make one G, H, I and J as cross sections of the neck and space them equally along the A's, then fix them in place with fine wire. Take the other G to form the tail, binding half the length to A and leaving the other half free. Bend K into the cross section of the nose and wire in position. Form L into the front view of the head with horns and ears. Secure in place to A's with fine wire.

Make M's into cross sections of the upper back legs and wire to C and D. Similarly bend N's into cross sections of the front upper legs and secure in place to B and D. Form the O's into cross sections of the front upper legs and wire to B and D's. Make P's, Q's, R's and S's into cross sections of the front and back legs, space them along B, C and D's and join them together with fine wire. Bend T to form the tail and wire to D's and G. Form U's into cross sections of the tail and secure to T and G.

Cover the framework with chicken wire. Start with the neck as it is a simple form and mould the mesh round the wire frame. Continue with the body, head and legs to cover the main part of the framework. Trim off surplus chicken wire to cover the horns and ears. Bend all the sharp wire ends out of harm's way behind the surface netting.

Lay strips of pasted paper in a lattice over the frame to form a foundation on which to build up the base coat of papier mâché. Cover the large areas with wide strips of paper and smaller curved sections with narrow strips. Build up to the required thickness and allow to dry thoroughly. Treat the surface with waterproofing liquid.

Prime the surface and then decorate the giraffe with exterior quality paint. Place it in the garden, avoiding exposed areas as its height makes it vulnerable in high winds. If necessary, the legs can be tethered to pegs and a fine nylon cord fixed round the neck and attached to a nearby tree for extra stability.

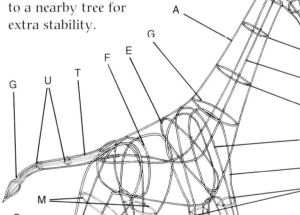

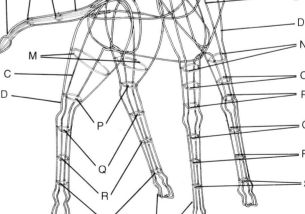

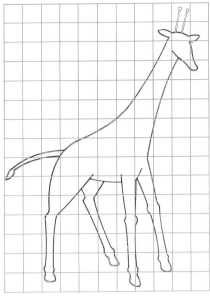

Each square represents 150mm (6 inches)

1 Form the shape of the head, ears and horns from length L. Use the combination pliers to grip and bend the wire into the desired configuration before securing in place.

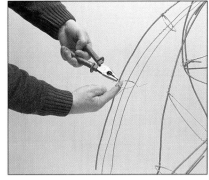

2 The tail is wired together using fine wire. Use combination pliers to twist the join tight, then neatly wind the surplus wire round the the frame to keep sharp ends out of the way.

3 Form the chicken wire round the tail frame by squeezing and bending the mesh to make a smooth shape. Fold over wire ends into the adjoining netting to secure firmly in place.

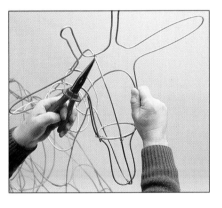

4 Twist wire joins tight to provide a firm joint to the framework. The long-nose pliers reach into the confined spaces where the narrow tips can grip the wire with ease.

5 The completed wire frame shows the splayed legs which helps the stability. Angles of legs, head and neck can be adjusted at this stage, should it be necessary, by bending the wire frame.

6 Bind strips of pasted paper round the horns like a bandage. Use narrow strips for covering the ends where the curve is more pronounced – this will avoid creases on the surface.

7 Use wide strips of paper on the legs as they cover the form quickly but use narrow strips round the hooves to give a smooth finish to the surface of the papier mâché.

8 To give a crisp edge to the spots use a fine pointed brush. Make the spots irregular in shape for a natural effect and be careful not to smudge any wet paint.

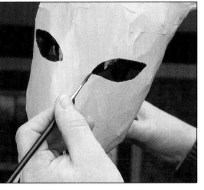

9 Sharp points, angles and fine lines on the face are best made with a fine brush. If the paint is thick and sticky, dilute with a little turps to allow the paint to run smoothly.

Making a
Papier Mâché
TIGER

A full-sized tiger is not the first thing that comes to mind when an animal for your garden is suggested, but it sure is a spectacular object of interest with its striped coat. Stretching some 2285mm (90in) long from nose to tail, the tiger isn't something that will just tuck out of sight behind a clump of flowers. Be bold – use it as a main focal point.

Bend one A to form the side view of the tiger's head, body and tail, then wire the overlapping wire together. From the other A make a plan view of the tiger and check that it fits to the first A before fixing together. Join at the head and tail where the frame crosses with fine wire. Make B into the front view of the forelegs with one leg stretched forward, wire to both A's. Bend one C to form the front view of the back legs with one leg stretched back and the other forward. Secure in place to the A's with fine wire. Make the other C into the plan view of the body alone and join to A's and B. Make the side appearance of the back legs from the two D's and check that they fit to the framework of A's and C's before wiring together. Form E's into the side views of the front legs and join to A's, B and C after checking that they fit together. Bend the cross sections of the body from F, G and H, then wire them to A's and C. Make I into the front view of the head with ears and secure

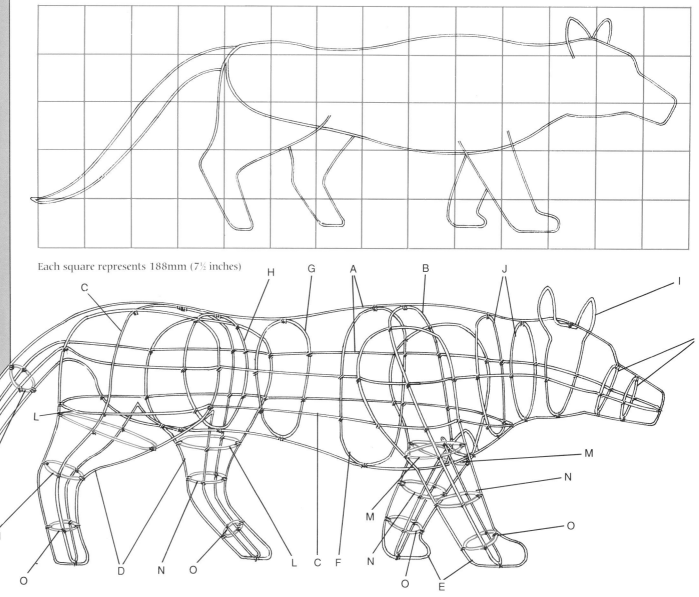

Each square represents 188mm (7½ inches)

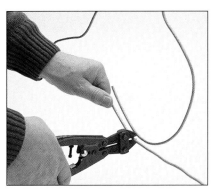

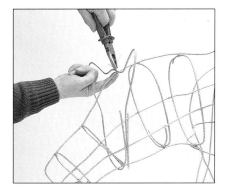

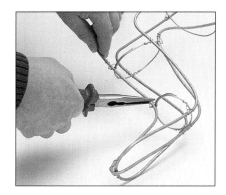

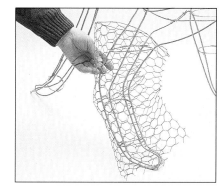

1 Cut the 4mm wire with powerful wire or bolt cutters. Form the front view of the head complete with ears from I, then bind the overlap with fine wire to secure.

2 Fix the head shape I to the frame with wire, use combination pliers to twist tight the tie, then neatly wrap the surplus fine wire round the adjoining frame.

3 Use the long-nose pliers to wind the surplus fine wire round the frame to place the sharp wire end tight against the frame to give a neat finish.

4 Partially prepare the form of the chicken wire and then place this round the leg. Squeeze and pull the mesh to fit it close to the frame then secure by bending the edges through the adjoining netting.

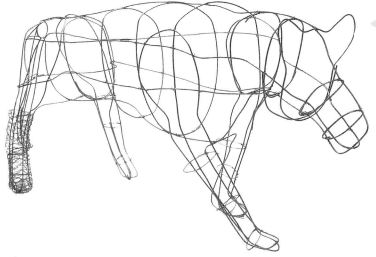

5 The completed tiger framework. At this stage you can adjust the stance and angles of the legs to make sure that it stands square on the ground and doesn't wobble.

6 Lay strips of pasted paper round the framework like a bandage and firm in place with the fingers. Cover the nose area with narrow strips to avoid creases on its small curves and tight forms.

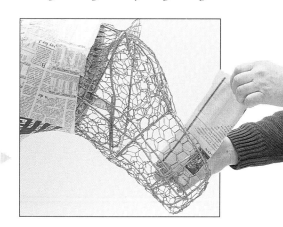

in place. Form the J's into cross sections of the neck, place in position and wire where the frame crosses. Bend the two K's into sections of the nose and fix in place with fine wire to A's. Make the two L's into cross sections of the back thighs and secure in place. Form the two M's into sections of the front upper leg and fix in position with wire. Bend the four N's into the middle sections of each leg and join to the framework with fine wire. Make the four O's into lower leg sections and fix to the framework of the legs. Form the three P's into sections of the tail and space out equally along the A's and wire in position.

Cover the framework with chicken wire. Start with the large piece for the body and continue to the extremities. Bend over all sharp wire edges as you proceed to avoid being scratched. Keep the forms smooth by pulling and squeezing the mesh into shape.

Lay strips of pasted paper over the framework: it is easier to build up a lattice work of strips round the body and then fill in the gaps. Continue to build up layers of papier mâché until the required thickness is reached and allow to dry thoroughly. Treat the surface with waterproofing liquid, following the manufacturer's instructions carefully.

Paint the surface of the tiger with primer and follow this with exterior-quality paint to provide it with its characteristic markings. Position the tiger in the garden as a focal point.

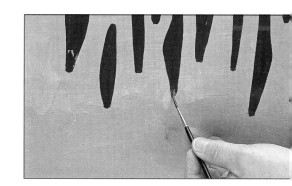

7 Paint with a fine brush to give sharp edges and clean pointed ends to the stripes. Take care not to overload the brush to avoid runs down the side of the tiger.

Making a
Papier Mâché
DINOSAUR

*T*here is a growing interest in dinosaurs that
is not confined just to children but encompasses
all ages. You can make one of these prehistoric
monsters to have as a domestic pet and display
it in the garden where it will surprise visitors.
This particular form is a Stegosaurus and is
chosen because of its interesting back plates
and tail spikes. Although the original beasts
were some 6–7 metres (20–25 ft) long, our
model is reduced to fit into an average garden.
They are made in three sections for ease of
making and moving. These can be left separate
or joined up permanently. You can display the
dinosaur in the open, or, to increase the sense of
mystery, half hide it behind some shrubs.

84

YOU WILL NEED

For ease of construction the model
is divided into three sections.

SECTION I – HEAD

4mm wire:
one length 4265mm (168in) (A)
one length 3660mm (144in) (B)
one length 2440mm (96in) (C)
one length 1065mm (42in) (D)
one length 1830mm (72in) (E)
one length 1220mm (48in) (F)
four lengths 915mm (36in) (G)
three lengths 610mm (24in) (H)
one length 455mm (18in) (I)

2mm wire:
one length 3050mm (120in) (J)
one length 2550mm (100in) (K)
one length 2285mm (90in) (L)
one length 1525mm (60in) (M)

.9mm wire:
various short lengths to tie the
frame together

chicken wire:
one piece 2440 x 915mm
(96 x 36in) body
one piece 1220 x 915mm
(48 x 36in) head
two pieces 915 x 405mm
(36 x 16in) back plates
three pieces 505 x 300mm
(20 x 12in) plates and jaw

Bend A into the side profile of the head and neck
and fold over the ends to make hooks. Form B
into the plan view and similarly bend the ends to
make hooks. Make C into the cross section of the
neck near the body and bind the overlap together
with fine wire. Position the hooks on A and B over
C, then pinch them tight and secure with wire.
Form D into the plan view of the lower jaw and fix
to A and B. Make E and F into the cross sections of
the body and wire them in place to A and B. Bend
one G and one H into cross sections of the body and
secure in place to A and B. Take another G and H to
form lateral supports and join to C and E with G,
continuing to F, and then wire in place. Form the
remaining G's into back plates and fix one in place
to the lateral G and the other to
the lateral H. Similarly take H
and I and form the other two
back plates and secure to A and
convenient cross sections of the
body. Make J, K, L and M into
cross sections of the back plates
and body, and then position
them on the framework and
secure them with fine wire
where the frame crosses.

Cover the completed framework with chicken wire, mould
the mesh carefully into place and
secure. Fold all sharp wire ends
behind the adjoining netting to

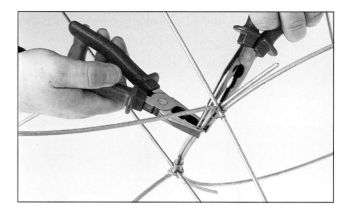

1 *Use two sets of pliers to bend the 4mm wire in confined
spaces. Here the wire is carefully bent to follow the main curve
of the frame and achieve a smooth form.*

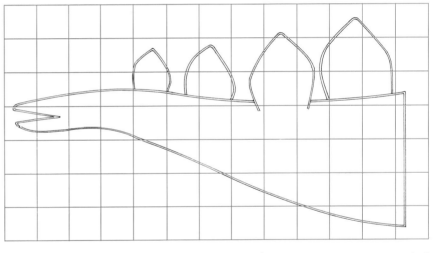

Each square represents 150mm (6 inches)

keep the surface as smooth as possible.

Stick strips of pasted paper over the framework
to build up the papier mâché covering. Use wide
strips of paper on the plain areas for speed and
ease. Once you reach the required thickness, leave
to dry. Spray the inside and outside with
waterproofing solution. Follow the manufacturer's
instructions for best results.

Prime the surface and decorate with exterior
quality paint. Use a wide brush to cover the large
areas and a smaller one for details.

Bend the A's into lengths of the body, folding over the ends to make hooks. Similarly, form four B's and the C's into lengths of the body. Make two B's into the cross sections of the body ends to match the head section. Position the hooks on A's, B's and C's over the two ends and pinch the hooks tight, then secure with fine wire. Form two B's, D and E's into cross sections of the body and fix to A's, B's and C's where the frame crosses. Bend the remaining two B's into front views of the legs and wire to A, B's and C's. Form F's into side views of the legs and secure to the C's where the frame crosses. Make G's into rings and fix to B's and F's. Bend H's into the back plates and wire to A's and convenient cross sections of the body.

Cover the framework with the chicken wire and papier mâché. Follow the instructions for the head section to complete this part.

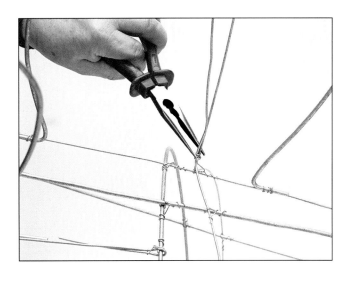

2 Tie the frame together with fine wire, twisting and winding the surplus round the frame. Use the long-nose pliers to squeeze tight the wire tips and keep the sharp ends safe.

YOU WILL NEED

SECTION II – BODY

4mm wire:
four lengths 2745mm (108in) (A)
eight lengths 2440mm (96in) (B)
two lengths 2135mm (84in) (C)
one length 3660mm (144in) (D)
two lengths 3050mm (120in) (E)
four lengths 1980mm (78in) (F)
eight lengths 815mm (32in) (G)
twelve lengths 1220mm (48in) (H)

.9mm wire:
various short lengths to tie the framework together

chicken wire:
one piece 3660 x 915mm
(144 x 36in) centre body
two pieces 3050 x 915mm
(120 x 36in) body ends
four pieces 815 x 200mm
(32 x 8in) legs
twelve pieces 915 x 405mm
(36 x 16in) back plates

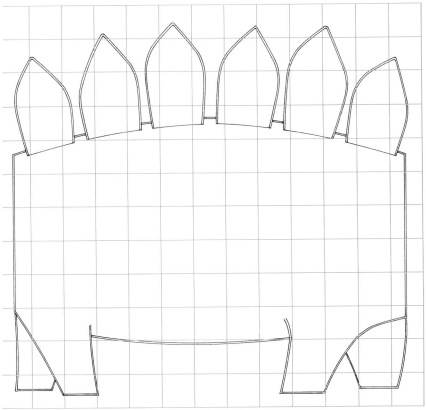

Each square represents 150mm (6 inches)

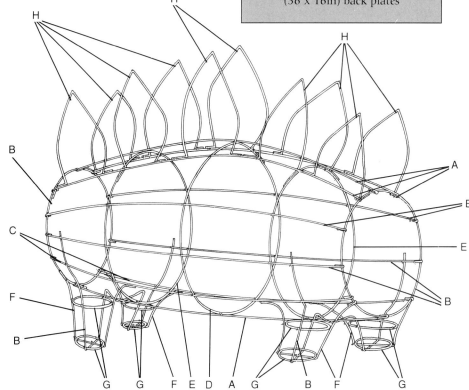

Bend the three A's into lengths of the tail, making sure that there is a sharp bend half way to make a pointed tip to the tail. Fold the ends over to make hooks. Form B into the cross section of the body end to the tail and matches the body section. Bind the overlap with fine wire. Position the hooks over B and pinch tight, then secure with wire. Make C, one D and E's into cross sections of the tail and fix in place to A's. Bend the back plates out of the two D's and F's, then wire in place to A's

and any nearby cross sections. Form the G's into spikes and fix to A's, D and E's.

Make H's and I's into rings and join to G's with fine wire. Cover the framework with chicken wire and follow the instructions for the head section to complete. You can either join all three sections or for ease of transport leave them separate and just butt them together. You can now place them in the garden and sit back and enjoy your very own pet dinosaur as it looms out of the foliage.

3 Fold the chicken wire over the back plate. Trim off surplus netting and bend the sharp wire ends out of harm's way under the adjacent mesh to make a neat edge.

4 Place the half-formed chicken wire over the spike frame and squeeze with the hand to mould the mesh to the frame. Fold over all loose wire ends to leave a smooth surface.

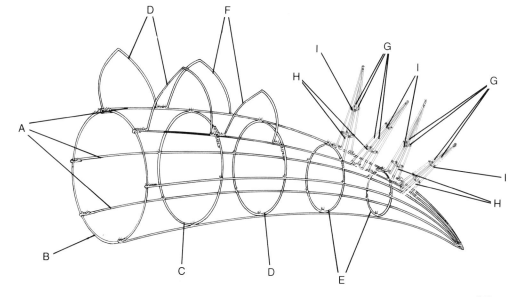

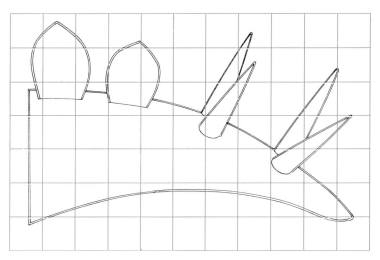

Each square represents 150mm (6 inches)

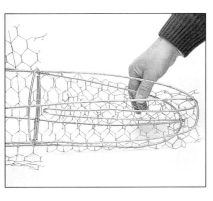

5 Cover the inside of the mouth by cutting the mesh and then folding the flaps in and securing. Use the diagonal cutting nippers to cut the surplus chicken wire off and remove.

6 Lay strips of pasted paper over the backplates to form the papier mâché covering. Firm in place with the fingers to ensure that there is good adhesion and no creases.

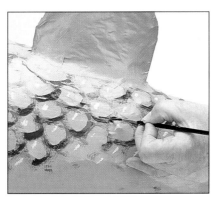

7 Wind strips of pasted paper round each spike like a bandage and firm in place. Stick narrow strips over the spike tips to make a smooth point without wrinkles.

8 Simulate the dinosaur's scales with paint – although it can look rough in close up, it appears far more natural from a distance. Use a fine brush to place the dark shadows.

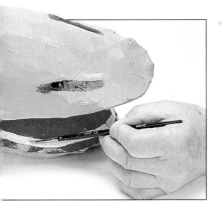

9 Paint the inside of the mouth with red and then draw a white line to represent the teeth. To give a clean sharp edge to the white line, use a fine pointed sable brush.

Making a
Papier Mâché
PIXIE

*C*reate a surprise in the garden and delight a child – hide this unexpected model from general view so that it is discovered when you turn a corner! This miniature figure appears to have stepped out of a fairy tale, dressed in bright clothes and seated in solitary splendour waiting to perform an act of mischief.

YOU WILL NEED

2mm wire:
one length 1065mm (42in) (A)
one length 2540mm (100in) (B)
two lengths 510mm (20in) (C)
one length 405mm (16in) (D)
five lengths 200mm (8in) (E)
two lengths 2030mm (80in) (F)
one length 1700mm (67in) (G)
two lengths 125mm (5in) (H)

.9mm wire:
various short lengths for tying
the frame together

chicken wire:
two pieces 300 x 300mm
(12 x 12in) back and front
one piece 150 x 405mm
(6 x 16in) head
two pieces 200 x 200mm
(8 x 8in) thigh
two pieces 150 x 175mm
(6 x 7in) upper arm
two pieces 200 x 230mm
(8 x 9in) lower leg
two pieces 125 x 175mm
(5 x 7in) lower arm
two pieces 100 x 125mm
(4 x 5in) feet

Form A into a profile of the head and body, taking care to mould the features, and then wire the ends together. Make the front elevation of the body complete with arms from B, join the ends together and fix to A with fine wire where the wire crosses top and bottom. Make the two C's into cross sections of the chest and waist, then wire to A and B. Carefully model D to form the cross section of the head, taking pains over the nose shape before you fix it to A and B. Form the section of the neck with one E and wire to A and B. With one F construct a plan view of the legs, making the wire go round the back of the body – bend the wire to give animation to the angles. Form the remaining F to make the profile of the legs, checking with the first F to make sure the frame will match in dimensions and angles. Position and secure with fine wire to A and B. Bend G into shape to form the profile of the arms and check with B to ensure that the whole fits together accurately before fixing to A and B. Form two of the remaining E's to make cross sections of each thigh and wire into place. Bend the two H's to form sections of each upper arm and secure to B and G. Take the last two E's and make the footshapes and wire these to the two F's.

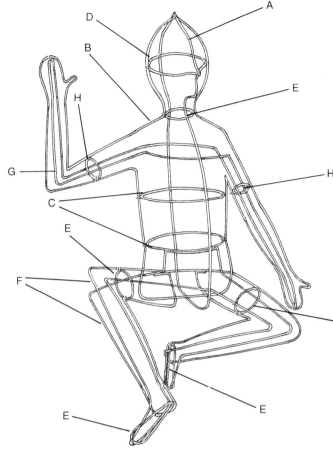

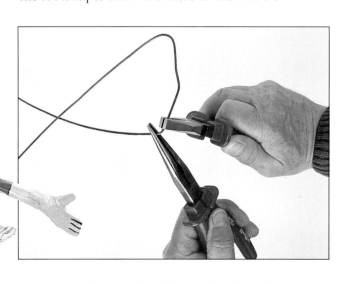

1 Starting with the profile of the head, length A is bent into shape. If you find the wire stiff to bend and for making sharp angles, use two sets of pliers to grip – the added leverage will make the task simple.

2 Some of the forms can be bound with pasted strips like a bandage. Here the foot is having a strip of paper wound round it. Finer forms will need narrower strips to cover the area without creasing.

Cover the frame with chicken wire, starting with the simple back shape and trimming off surplus mesh where necessary. Continue with the covering, working from the simple forms to those that need more modelling. Bend over all the sharp ends as you proceed.

Build up layers of papier mâché on the completed framework. Form the hat brim with strips of paper laid in place and joined to the head at the lower edge. Allow to dry thoroughly before treating with the waterproofing compound. Follow the manufacturer's instructions exactly. When dry, apply a coat of primer, and when this has dried, the various top coats. Use a fine brush for details of features and buttons. All that you need now is a suitable location to seat the completed pixie and await the reaction from children of all ages.

3 Larger areas of the figure are painted with exterior quality paint, taking care where they butt against each other. Use a soft-haired brush which will give a sharp edge to the patch of colour.

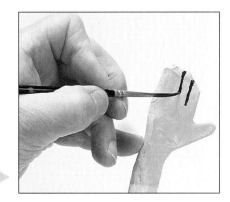

4 For fine details use a small pointed brush that will give a thin crisp line. ▶

MONKEY &
BANANA

*B*ring a little fun into the
garden with a swinging
monkey, complete with
a half-peeled banana.
Easily hooked over a
convenient branch, it
will swing in the breeze,
bringing delight to both
children and adults. You
can use this model either as an
eye-catching focal point or as a
simple surprise that springs on the unwary as
they wander into a screened area of the garden.

94

YOU WILL NEED

FOR THE MONKEY

4mm wire:
one length 4570mm (180in) (A)
one length 3300mm (130in) (B)
one length 1775mm (70in) (C)
one length 1015mm (40in) (D)
one length 1525mm (60in) (E)
one length 1625mm (64in) (F)
two lengths 1320mm (52in) (G)
one length 1120mm (44in) (H)
one length 915mm (36in) (I)
one length 710mm (28in) (J)
one length 635mm (25in) (K)
one length 455mm (18in) (L)

2mm wire:
two lengths 405mm (16in) (M)
two lengths 300mm (12in) (N)
two lengths 250mm (10in) (O)
two lengths 380mm (15in) (P)
four lengths 275mm (11in) (Q)

.9mm wire:
various short lengths to tie the
frame together

chicken wire:
one piece 610 x 1120mm
(24 x 44in) body
one piece 300 x 870mm
(12 x 34in) head
two pieces 380 x 915mm
(15 x 36in) arms
two pieces 405 x 635mm
(16 x 25in) legs

FOR THE BANANA

2mm wire:
one length 1015mm (40in) (A)
one length 915mm (36in) (B)
one length 200mm (8in) (C)

.9mm wire:
various short lengths to tie the
frame together

Form A into the front view of the monkey with the lower arm and legs bent forward for a natural look. Ensure that you make one of the hands curved to hook over a branch and the other bent to hold a banana. Make B into the side view of the upper arm, body and one leg. Join together at the hand and bottom with fine wire. Bend C into the side appearance of the head and body, wire to A at the top of the head and bottom. Form D to be the side elevation of the body and fix to A at the shoulder and bottom. Make E into the side view of the leg and wire to A and D. Bend F to make the plan shape of the leg, matching this to E for the dimensions and angles, then securing it in place to A, C, D and E. Form one G into the plan view of the other leg and fix to A, B and C. Make the other G into the plan shape of the lower arm and wire to A and D. Curve H to make the cross section of the chest and wire in place to A, B, C and D. Bend I to form the waist section and wire to A, B, C and D. Form J to be the cross section of the head level with the eyebrows, while K makes the section through at mouth level. Secure J and K to A and C with fine wire. Curve L to be the cross section of the neck and fix in place to A and C. Make M's, N's and O's into leg sections and wire into position to A, B and E. Bend P's and Q's into cross sections of the arms and secure in place to A, B and G with fine wire. Hang the framework up in position and bend or twist any limb to give a good balanced shape.

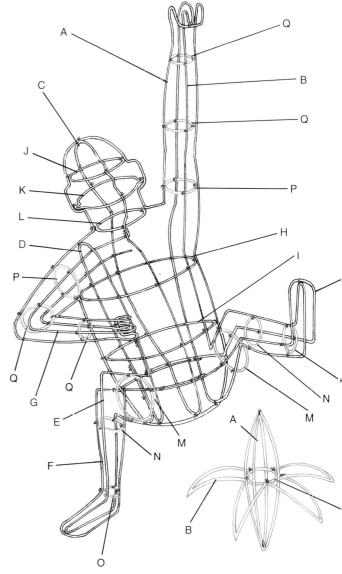

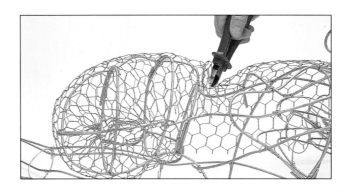

1 Fold the netting under the chin. Surplus mesh is cut off using the diagonal cutting nippers. Bend the wire ends under the adjacent chicken wire out of the way.

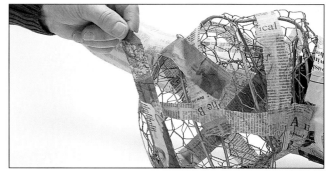

2 Lay a lattice of pasted paper strips over the head frame to hold the covering of papier mâché in place, then fill the gaps with more paper to complete the base coat.

Cover the framework with chicken wire. Start with the simple forms and as you progress you will find it easier with the more complicated forms. Bend all the sharp wires out of the way as you work towards completion.

Lay strips of pasted paper over the completed framework. Form a lattice of strips to hold the papier mâché in position as you work. Continue to place layers of paper until you reach the required thickness. Allow to dry before applying the waterproofing solution.

Prime the surface, and then follow this with exterior-quality paint to decorate the monkey in the colours of your choice. Use a fine pointed brush for the details of the hands, feet and the facial features.

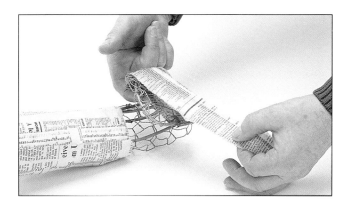

3 Position strips of paper round the hand to cover it. The hand forms the hook that the monkey hangs from and so this needs a good coat of papier mâché to stand wear and tear.

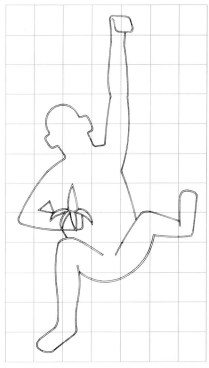

Each square represents 100mm (4 inches)

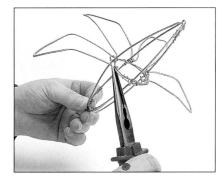

4 Use a fine pointed brush to paint the details, such as fingers and features. The long hairs provide a clean edge to the stroke and the point allows fine detail to be applied.

5 Use the long-nose pliers to reach into confined spaces to grip the fine wire ties. Twist the wire tight and wrap the surplus round the adjoining framework.

6 Wrap the pasted paper strip round the peeled banana 'leaves' and firm down with the fingers to give a smooth surface. Continue until you reach the required thickness.

7 Colour the banana with its characteristic yellow livery. Paint additional details using a fine pointed brush. Use the little finger as a support to steady the hand for fine detail.

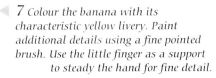

Carefully bend A to form the banana shape 230mm (9in) long, using pliers to make the crisp angles at both ends, and then wire together with fine wire. Form B into four 'leaves' of half-peeled banana skin 115mm (4½in) long and curved to give a natural appearance. Make C into the cross section of the banana and wire this in place to A. Now wire B to A and C to complete the banana framework.

This model has no chicken wire: the papier mâché is applied directly over the framework. Build up the layers of paper to the desired thickness and allow to dry. Treat with the waterproofing solution.

Prime the surface and cover in suitable exterior-quality paints. Place the banana in the monkey's hand and hang him on an appropriate branch.

Making a
Papier Mâché
GARDENER
& ROBIN

*M*ost garden benches spend their time empty, looking decidedly vacant and crying out to be occupied. To satisfy this need and to give the garden an occupied appearance, why not make your own gardener? True, he is very passive, even lazy, but he ensures that the seat is in use. To give an added sparkle a robin can be made to sit upon a spade or a fork handle. Although the instructions look daunting, if you take each step one at a time it will turn out to be quite simple.

You Will Need

FOR THE GARDENER

4mm wire:
one length 2160mm(85in) (A)
two lengths 3555mm (140in) (B)
one length 2440mm (96in) (C)
one length 1370mm (54in) (D)
two lengths 1120mm (44in) (E)
one length 4060mm (160in) (F)
three lengths 550mm (22in) (G)
two lengths 665mm (26in) (H)
four lengths 610mm (24in) (I)
two lengths 760mm (30in) (J)
two lengths 300mm (12in) (K)

2mm wire:
one length 1625mm (64in) (L)
two lengths 430mm (17in) (M)
one length 1170mm (46in) (N)
two lengths 610mm (24in) (O)
one length 710mm (28in) (P)
five lengths 300mm (12in) (Q)
two lengths 760mm (30in) (R)

chicken wire:
one piece 815 x 175mm
(32 x 7in) head
two pieces 815 x 355mm
(32 x 14in) back and chest
one piece 915 x 200mm
(36 x 8in) waist
two pieces 665 x 300mm
(26 x 12in) thighs
two pieces 610 x 510mm
(24 x 20in) lower legs
two pieces 300 x 300mm
(12 x 12in) feet

Make A into the side of the head and body. As most of it will be covered with a handkerchief you need not be over critical with the detail. Wire the two ends together. Bend one B into a side view of the body and leg but minus the head. Check with the chosen seat to obtain the correct angles and dimensions and adjust the wire to fit exactly. Repeat the shape with the other B and wire the ends together. Form C to make the front view of the head and body.

Fit A, B's and C together, tying with the fine wire where the frame crosses. Make D into the chest and arm cross section and wire into place. Bend one E to make the waist section and secure to A, B's and C with wire. The remaining E is made into the base of the bottom and wired into its position. Form F into the plan view of the legs, checking that the angles and measurements fit with the two B's. Fit into place and wire to A, B's and C. Bend one G to make the neck section and wire into

position to A and C. Use the two G's to form the knee sections and secure to B's and F. Form the two H's to make thigh sections and fix to B's and F, follow with the I's, which make the calf sections, and fit into place using fine wire.

Make the two J's into feet shapes and wire to B's and F. Bend the two K's to form heel extensions and wire to F. Construct the handkerchief with L forming the perimeter and the two M's as cross pieces; bend the ends of both M's round L to form a 380mm (15in) square. Check that this fits to the head but do not secure until the head is covered with chicken wire. Use N to make the front of the arms from shoulder to shoulder via the hands and fix this to the torso with wire. Form the backs of the arms to the elbows with the two O's and wire in place. Mould P to link between the two O's and form the lower edge of the forearms, secure in position. Bend the three Q's to make arm sections and attach them to the O's and P. Form the two R's

1 When joining the framework with fine wire, carefully wrap the surplus round the thicker wire. Use pliers to twist the fine wire tightly, placing the sharp end hard against the frame.

2 Form the chicken wire round the head leaving the crown uncovered. Here the handkerchief framework is placed over the head to show how much mesh is necessary, the surplus being trimmed off.

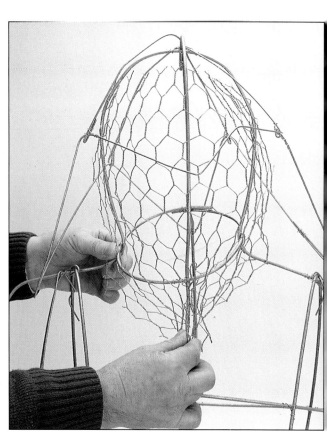

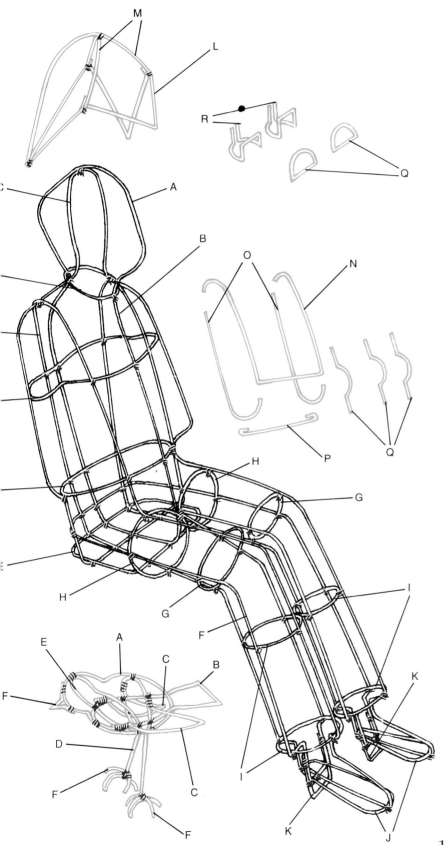

3 Start the second layer of papier mâché using white paper which shows up on the base coat of tinted paper. Leave the strips of paper to soak up the paste before spreading over the figure and smoothing.

4 Covering the handkerchief with papier mâché, building it up from the edge. Take care in the early stages as the covering is delicate and vulnerable, easily damaged and pierced. It becomes tougher as the additional layers are applied.

101

into heels for the boots and wire them to B's, F, J's and K's. Bend the two Q's into cross sections of the shoes and fix in place. Check the whole figure with the seat to make sure everything fits properly.

Cover the frame with chicken wire, it is best to start with the simple shapes first and gradually work to those areas where more modelling is needed. Bend all sharp ends under as you continue to cover the figure. Once the model is covered, take the handkerchief formed from L and the two M's and fold it over the head for a natural look and temporarily tie it into place.

Remove the handkerchief and using strips of paper cover the head but leave some of the chicken wire exposed on top of the head for anchorage. When there is sufficient thickness of papier mache spread over the lower half of the head, the wire frame of the handkerchief can be refixed. Lay strips over L and M's, working from corner to corner – as it has no chicken wire it will give a fine smooth finish but it will be vulnerable to damage while it is wet. Continue with the rest of the figure until the whole is completed and allow it to dry before applying the waterproofing.Brush a coat of primer over the surface and follow with coats of exterior quality paint to simulate the clothes and flesh.

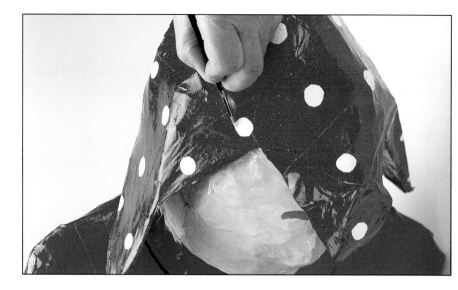

5 *Painting the completed and waterproofed papier mâché takes a little attention. Use a generously sized brush for the large areas but for small patches, lines and details use a fine brush that will give crisp edge.*

Bend A into the side view of the robin's head and body but excluding the beak and tail, then wire the ends together. Shape B into the plan view of the body and tail and join the ends with fine wire. The two C's make the wing shapes, but leave the free ends until the bird is formed and then model the wires to the bird's contours. Make D into the cross section of the back with the legs, bending the wire to form the centre claw and spur. Wire A, B and D together and follow with the two C's. Form E into the front view of the head and breast and wire into place. Bend one E to form the beak and mould the surplus wire to follow the line of the head and fix in position. The other two E's make the remaining claws and are wired to D.

Cover the head and body of the robin with chicken wire, taking care to model the forms and twisting the sharp wire ends out of the way.

Build up the coats of papier mache to the correct thickness leaving the legs bare to emphasise how slender they are. Treat the dried papier mache with the waterproofing liquid to seal the surface before the primer is applied. Using exterior paint, cover the bird to form the desired effect. Once dry, the gardener and his robin can be moved to their positions and left to amuse the onlooker.

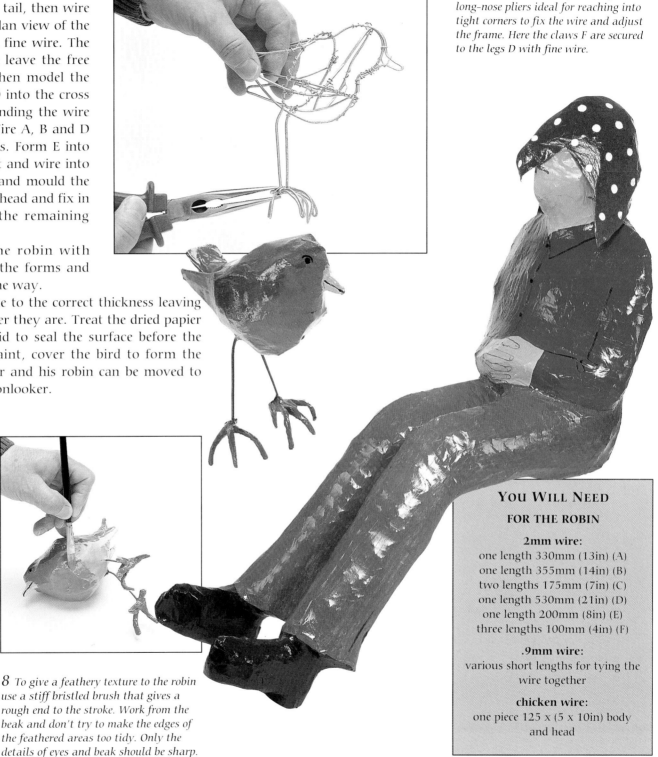

6 In making the robin you will find the long-nose pliers ideal for reaching into tight corners to fix the wire and adjust the frame. Here the claws F are secured to the legs D with fine wire.

7 For small forms narrow strips of pasted paper are used to make the papier mâché, tiny shapes such as the claws and beak use small scraps of torn paper to cover them. Note that the legs are left uncovered.

8 To give a feathery texture to the robin use a stiff bristled brush that gives a rough end to the stroke. Work from the beak and don't try to make the edges of the feathered areas too tidy. Only the details of eyes and beak should be sharp.

YOU WILL NEED

FOR THE ROBIN

2mm wire:
one length 330mm (13in) (A)
one length 355mm (14in) (B)
two lengths 175mm (7in) (C)
one length 530mm (21in) (D)
one length 200mm (8in) (E)
three lengths 100mm (4in) (F)

.9mm wire:
various short lengths for tying the wire together

chicken wire:
one piece 125 x (5 x 10in) body and head

Making a
Papier Mâché
OLD LADY & BLACKBIRD

A garden seat often looks bare when not in use, especially if it is in view of the house. To give interest to and enhance the bench, a seated figure of an elderly lady reading is used. The old lady is made with a detachable head which can be rotated and tilted, as well as allowing a flower pot to sit within the hat brim. You can ring the changes of plants through the seasons so that she always has a floral display as headgear. An additional interest is provided with a separate blackbird that can either stand on the seat, or the back or the arm of the bench.

104

Although this model looks complicated to make, it is surprisingly simple if you take it step-by-step. The actual forms are easy to construct and the painting will cover up odd malformations which could give her extra character. Made life-sized it will give untold pleasure and interest to the garden scene.

Carefully bend one A to make the profile of the head with the addition of the neck 75mm (3in) long and 125mm (5in) in diameter, do take pains in shaping the nose. The surplus wire above the hat level is bent outwards for 75mm (3in) and then sideways to partially form and support the hat brim. The other A makes the front view of the head, working in conjunction with the first A to make a good head shape. Take B and bend into the cross section of the head from the nose to the back of the skull, join the wire at the back or side where it will not interfere with the nose form. Wire the two A's and B together where the wires cross. Form the top

1 Twist the wire on the head frame, using long-nose pliers to turn the sharp end of the fine wire under and combination pliers to grip the frame. This is particularly advised where there is little room for larger pliers or the frame is unsecured.

of the head from C using a large tin to form a circular section, check that the chosen flower pot fits loosely and make the ring oversize to allow for additional wire, chicken wire and papier mâché to encroach into the space. This is wired into place using the fine wire. Make D into the neck section and secure into position. Finally bend E round a convenient sized tin or drum, wire the ends together and then join to the ends of the A's.

Take the larger piece of chicken wire and mould it round the head, allowing the lower edge to cover the part of the neck and spreading the top edge to form part of the lower edge of the hat brim. Take care to form the features of the face to stay in character with the body of the old lady – an apple-cheeked plump head will not fit a slender lower form nor a roly poly figure go with an emaciated head. The hat brim is now covered with mesh; to make it easier to handle you can cut the length into sections and fold the surplus into the inside, as well as bending it over the brim itself. All sharp ends must be turned in to make a smooth and safe surface.

Cover the head and hat brim with papier mâché to the required thickness. Do some additional modelling to accentuate the facial features if

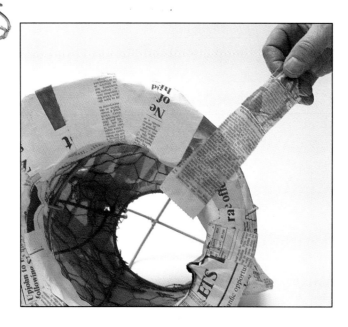

2 Mould the chicken wire round the wire frame of the head using the fingers and then trim off the surplus mesh round the neck area with the cutting nippers. Turn the wire ends of the mesh under the framework with pliers as you progress to prevent scratching.

3 The head receives its second coat of papier mâché. The strips are laid with one end stuck to the interior, run across the brim and then folded over the outside edge to reach under the brim and down the face. Watch for wrinkles on the inside of the head – if this occurs use narrower strips of paper.

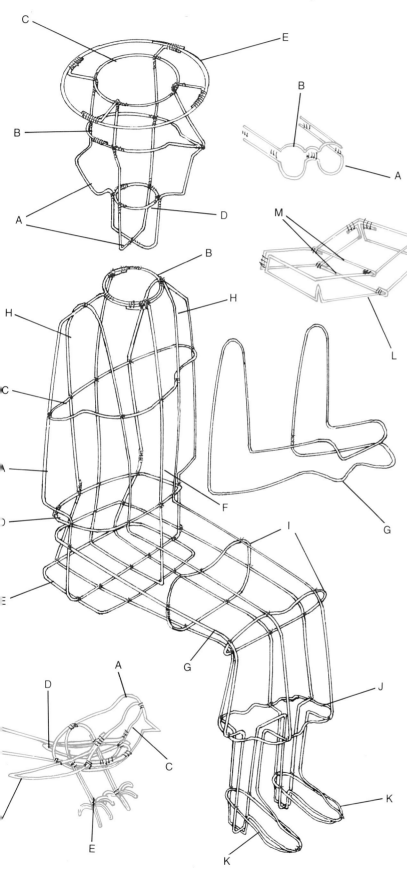

needed, but the overall impression is more important than tiny detail. Cover the neck with papier mâché where visible and also line the interior of the hat brim to give it strength.

Once the papier mâché is dry the waterproofing treatment is undertaken, with additional coats to the interior to protect against enthusiastic watering. Treat the whole head with primer and when dry the flesh, hair and hat brim are covered with exterior paint. Follow this with the details of the eyes, mouth, nose and ears.

Make the glasses in two parts. Bend A to form the bridge, lower half of the lenses and the arms, and with B make the top half. Check that both A and B fit together and join with fine wire round the bridge and both ends of the arms. Spray with metal primer and follow with a black top coat. Once dry fit the glasses to the head; the spring in the wire will hold them in place.

YOU WILL NEED

GLASSES

2mm wire:
one length 455mm (18in) (A)
one length 405mm (16in) (B)

.9mm wire:
short lengths for tying the wire together

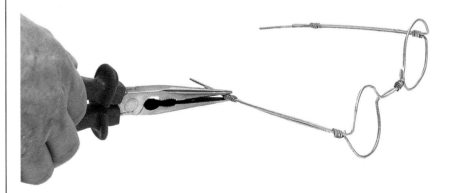

4 The two sections of the glasses A and B are joined together with fine wire along the arms and across the bridge. Note that the slight curve of the arms will give sufficient grip to hold the glasses in place.

YOU WILL NEED

BODY

4mm wire:
one length 2080mm (82in) (A)
one length 550mm (22in) (B)
one length 1120mm (44in) (C)
one length 915mm (36in) (D)
one length 1270mm (50in) (E)
one length 1575mm (62in) (F)
two lengths 3200mm (126in) (G)
two lengths 3425mm (135in) (H)
two lengths 870mm (34in) (I)
one length 1015mm (40in) (J)
two lengths 550mm (22in) (K)

2mm wire:
one length 2080mm (82in) (L)
two lengths 250mm (10in) (M)

.9mm wire:
various short lengths for tying
the frame together

chicken wire:
one piece 550 x 550mm
(22 x 22in) back
one piece 510 x 610mm
(20 x 24in) front
one piece 610 x 455mm
(24 x 18in) back of skirt
one piece 610 x 610mm
(24 x 24in) front of skirt
one piece 300 x 300mm
(12 x 12in) fore arms
one piece 300 x 550mm
(12 x 22in) book
two pieces 300 x 405mm
(12 x 16in) legs
two pieces 250 x 230mm
(10 x 9in) feet

Take A and bend into shape of the front view of the torso, including the upper arms, and then wire ends together. Form B round a tin to make a ring larger than the neck of the head in order for it to drop in with space for the chicken wire and papier mâché that is going to be applied later. Wire B to the top of A, ensuring that the curves are compatible, so A will not foul the neck when it is placed in. Form C to shape and secure in place, then wire to A. Similarly make D and fix in position. Take E and form to shape – make sure that it fits the base of A where it is joined with fine wire. Bend F to form the sides of the torso; the two ends are bent at right angles to fit along B. Wire all places where the frame wires cross. Construct the arms from one G: bend the wire to make the arms look right for reading a book. Secure G in place to A and C. Form one side of the seated figure, including the legs and feet from one H.

It is wise at this point to check with the chosen seat or bench to make sure all the angles and dimensions will fit. Fit H to the torso and once you are satisfied, use H to repeat the shape on the remaining H. Fix both H's in place using the fine wire. Bend the other G round the back and then form the front view of the legs, checking with H's

for the angles and skirt length. Place in position and use fine wire to secure. Make one I a cross section of the lap and fix in place. Follow this with the other I which makes the cross section of the knees. Bend J to make the undulating hem of the skirt and then fix to G and H's with fine wire. Make the plan views of the feet with the two K's and wire in place. Bend L to form the book wire together and add M's to make the spine. Bend the ends over L and fix in place, then secure to the arms G with fine wire.

Check the completed wire frame and make sure it sits comfortably on the desired seat before the chicken wire is fixed. Start with the back and fit the mesh, trim off surplus wire where necessary, then follow with the other large pieces that cover simple forms. As you proceed to more complicated forms, do bend all the sharp ends out of the way and keep the surface smooth and even. Check that the head still fits easily.

Cover the completed framework with layers of papier mâché until the desired thickness is reached. Make holes in the base of the body and feet to allow any surplus moisture, from watering the flower pot, to drain away. Check that the head fits and moves in the required directions. Once the papier mâché is dry, treat the whole figure with

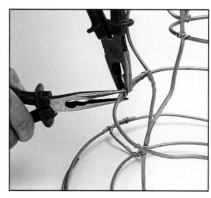

5 *Wiring the body frame together securing F to A and B. Use the long-nose pliers to twist the fine wire round to grip the 4mm framework.*

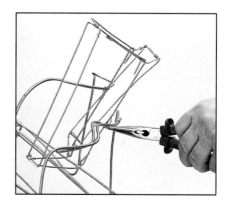

6 *The book, made from L, is attached to the arms and hand framework G with long-nosed pliers. Try to keep all the wire work neatly bent round the frame as you advance. Adjust the angle of the book at this stage.*

7 *The second layer of white papier mâché is laid in strips over the base coat of coloured paper and rubbed down with the fingers to push out air bubbles. Make sure that the paper pasted is stuck without wrinkles to give a clean, smooth surface to the book.*

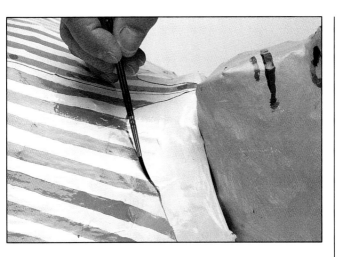

8 Use a thin brush to add the fine detail on the finished body. Slight imperfections give character to the figure and make the clothes look naturally crumpled and creased.

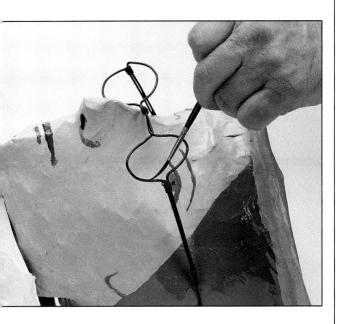

9 The final touches make the head look more realistic: the glasses are painted black to contrast with the flesh colour, to be seen at a distance and to add character.

waterproofing solution, making sure that the interior is well soaked for protection. Allow to dry thoroughly. Paint the surface with primer and follow with top coats of exterior paint to make the figure look dramatic.

Bend A to form the side view of the body and head exclude the tail then tie the wire ends together. Shape B to make the plan view of the body and tail, wire the ends together and join to A, wire in place where the wires cross on the breast. Form C to make front view of head and body of bird, wire ends and secure to A and B. Make the wings from the two D's and wire in place. Construct the legs and back from E, carefully bending the claws to grip onto a seat back or to stand free. Fix into position and check that the bird will balance – adjust if necessary by bending the angle of the legs. Use oddments of chicken wire to cover the framework, tuck all the sharp ends in and make the surface smooth to take the papier mâché.

Cover the surface of the bird with papier mâché to the required thickness and allow to dry. Bind the legs and claws with paper to give a smooth finish. Waterproof all the papier mâché with the solution, following the manufacturer's instructions.

Prime the bird before applying the top coats and adding the details of the bird's characteristic livery.

YOU WILL NEED

BLACKBIRD

2mm wire:
one length 455mm (18in) (A)
one length 510mm (20in) (B)
one length 380mm (15in) (C)
two lengths 250mm (10in) (D)
one length 1220mm (48in) (E)

.9mm wire:
short lengths for tying frame together

chicken wire:
odd pieces to cover head, body and tail

10 You will find the long-nose pliers ideal for working in confined spaces such as this blackbird framework. The fine wire ties the frame together and the pliers grip and manipulate the wire with ease, twisting the sharp ends out of harm's way.

11 The final details of eye and beak of the blackbird are added with a fine brush for accurate control. The eyes need careful positioning to give the bird its typical appearance.